And God Said . . .

OTHER WORKS BY THE AUTHOR

POETRY

The Heart Knows

Walking the Gunnysack Trail:
A Mountain Journey In Poetry

FICTION

Called: The Story of a Mountain Midwife

Millennium

NONFICTION

Catch a Falling Star:
The Stories That Test Scores Don't Tell

And God Said . . .

(A New Look at Ten Very Old Commandments)

PHYLLIS STUMP

2011

Parson's Porch Books Cleveland, Tennessee

Parson's Porch Books
121 Holly Trail Road, NW
Cleveland, Tennessee 37311

And God Said . . . (A New Look at Ten Very Old Commandments)

Published 2011.
Printed in the United States of America.
ISBN 978-1-936912-04-9

To order additional copies of this book, contact:

Parson's Porch Books
1-423-475-7308
www.parsonsporch.com

TABLE OF CONTENTS

PROLOGUE

IT'S A GORGEOUS SPRING DAY and I'm walking an old logging road that adjoins the Blue Ridge Parkway in Virginia. At some point I find myself blazing a trail that meanders away from the visible path, climbing towards a yet undiscovered view of the valley below. Golden-tinted leaves peak out from the trees overhead, not yet ready to reveal their varied and distinct shapes and hues. I'm searching for glimpses of flame azaleas, as I have earlier noted traces of their brilliant teasing of yellow, orange, and bright red shining through the green pines that reach so far into the sky that their tops cannot be seen.

Suddenly I stand face to face with a blazing mass of color so deep, so red, so "on fire" I am overcome with emotion. Then without a warning, a voice calls my name.

"Seek and ye shall find, Phyllis."

Oh, oh. My wanderings have finally gotten me into trouble. I have my trusty walking stick, but Princess, my faithful adopted dog, has taken off to chase a rabbit, and in spite on warnings by both neighbors, friends back home, and my husband, I am not carrying the ubiquitous cell phone. The voice seems to have come from behind me, or from the bush in front of me, or was it from the side of me, where the pine grove is dense and filled with unknowns. I slowly turn almost completing a circle, willing myself to confront whatever intruder has threatened my mountain sanctity. For over six years, I have done my share of staking off walking paths in all four directions up and down the hills that surround our mountain home. I have encountered local farmers, lost vacationers, UPS and FedEx drivers, motorcyclists who wave through the trees, fellow walkers (not many), some characters of dubious fame, one old man who offered me a tractor ride to see his log house up on another ridge, not to mention another older man who stopped in a truck telling me he was looking for someone he was supposed to meet on the Parkway but he could supply neither the destination nor the person's name. After leaving, he returned in about fifteen minutes to find me going in the opposite direction. Slowing down, he asked, "Need a ride?"

"Don't think so," I replied, "my husband's waiting for me to come and fix lunch. The house is just up the road." Not quite the truth, but it sufficed. He moved on, still looking for that someone he was supposed to meet somewhere for whatever purpose. He wouldn't tell.

My slow circle of discovery reveals no one. Is he hiding in the pine forest, I wonder or am I hallucinating? Since my mini-stroke, any and all events that I cannot explain, I attribute to a vein bursting in my brain.

"Are you searching for something in particular?" Strangely enough, the voice seems to be coming from the azalea bush. My mouth is shut dumb, which is highly unusual for an English teacher.

"You're always searching, aren't you, Phyllis? I've been watching you, you know, and listening, too. I take note of all those little prayers of yours while you're walking. I like the spontaneity, the way you see what so many others miss. Just like now.

You were looking for a flame azalea and you were willing to get off the beaten track to find one. Robert Frost would be proud of you; in fact, it's not a matter of 'would be'. He is, you know."

"He is? How do you know that?" I can't believe I'm standing in front of a blooming plant, talking to it as if it were a real person. Right now, I'm wishing I had my trusty cell phone in my hand and where has Princess gone anyway? Surely by now, she's tired of chasing that rabbit and is looking for me. Of course, this is a dog that is totally fearful of strangers. How she came to attach herself to me is beyond the comprehension of those who come to visit. But she does bark when strangers come to the house. She would bark to protect me, wouldn't she? Then again, how would a dog know to bark at someone or something she cannot see? But they do, I know. I hear her as she walks beside me, barking at something in the trees, in the grass, over the hill. If Princess could find me, I am convinced, she would rescue me.

"Of course she would." The voice is calm, reassuring.

"Would what?" I'm hoping this is a dream, so that I will soon wake up and say to Bob in the immortal words he has memorized, "I had the weirdest dream." And he will answer in his own immortal words, "You always have weird dreams."

"Of course she would rescue you and Bob is right; you do have weird dreams, but they tell a lot about you. We're getting off the subject, however. I suppose you are wondering why I am here, speaking to you in the form of a flame azalea."

"The thought has crossed my mind, although I must admit that I am having trouble processing the moment, if You are who I think You are. Then again," I add weakly, "You know all that anyway, don't you?" I am feeling slightly disoriented. Perhaps I am getting the flu.

"No, I am not the flu, Phyllis. I am Who you think I am; it's just hard for most humans to comprehend that I do, indeed, reveal myself to people like yourself, who are inclined to listen."

"I see," I reply, but honestly, I am still looking at the flame azalea with great doubts running through my mind.

"It's the burning bush, just like the one Moses saw in your Old Testament, though it's not exactly the same plant. Different climate, different environment, but the same concept, you understand."

"So . . ."

"Why am I here, today, speaking to you, in this place, and for what purpose?"

"You're very good with the Socratic Method, you know? You already know the answers to the questions you're asking, but you give your pupils a chance to come up with the answers," I stutter, but keep on going. "I must sound like an idiot. On the other hand, I suppose most of us do when we try to communicate with You, with our limited understanding." I am feeling totally helpless, trying to make sense of this utterly bizarre situation.

"I know you are feeling helpless and this is, I admit, a quite bizarre circumstance. A stronger word than situation, I think. I know how important finding the very best word is for you."

"You took the words right out of my mind. Oh, dear, I don't mean to be glib with You, of all people, God. That is if you are a people." I am handling this very poorly, I think to myself.

"Well, in a way, I am a people; in fact, a sum of all peoples, if that makes sense at all to you. As far as handling this poorly, it's been my experience in all the eons that I've had to deal with my creation, that aside from my dear Son, every one that I've had to deal with has fallen into the category of handling the idea of God very poorly. It's quite difficult, you understand, to be the CEO, as it were, of such a dysfunctional organization. Not that I should complain. I brought it all on myself, for better or worse, through sickness and in health, richer or poorer. You know where I'm coming from, I'm sure. The whole idea of marriage explains it more clearly than anything else that comes to mind."

"Thanks for the insight, but . . ."

"Why you? Why here? Why now?"

"All of the above."

"If you don't mind, I'll start with the last question and work backwards."

"Please, it's Your show. You can do anything you want."

"Thanks for the affirmation. You wouldn't believe how many human beings don't get that concept at all. They're always placing conditions, and limitations on my behavior, as in: 'God doesn't, blah, blah, blah; God won't, blah, blah, blah; God didn't, blah, blah, blah; God can't blah, blah, blah . . .' It goes on and on. To be honest with you, it really gets to me. And to be honest, Phyllis, one of the things that bothers me the most, is that so many of my dear sons and daughters think that the Creator has no sense of humor and, therefore, believe that they have no right to have one either. As if I could possibly watch over all the shenanigans going on down there and not have a good laugh now and then. On the other hand, I do a lot of crying as well. Much more of the crying, I will admit. Luckily, clouds are more common in heaven than Kleenex so I manage to keep my emotions under control."

I must have looked numb or stunned or bewildered or any combination thereof.

"Blah, blah, blah? I can't imagine that You would utter something so, so . . . inarticulate!"

"Just a joke, Phyllis. Now for the answers to your previous questions. I'm going to get straight to the point. Why now, at this moment, April 10, 2008, is God speaking to you, Phyllis Stump, at this place, a plowed field, adjoined by a pine forest, on the crest of the Blue Ridge Mountains in Virginia? It's this simple. Over six thousand years have gone by since I got Moses's attention with a burning bush, set him on the road to delivering the rules for living to a group of nomads that I chose to be "my people." You know the rest of that story, most of it comprising one disaster after another, even as I sent messenger after messenger into the melee, hoping that along the way, the light would break through, "my people" (as opposed to "their people") would get it, the world would head in an entirely new direction, etc. I won't go into all the details. You know something about the Old Testament, or the Hebrew Bible, whatever people want to call it. You've been a Sunday school teacher.

"So, four thousand years go by. The progress reports are not pretty. I decide to send my Son to get the mess straightened out. You also know the story. He shows up, first as a precious little baby boy, born to very devout parents. Grows up to be a fine Jewish young man, good-looking, smart, charismatic, some would say, a simple man preaching a simple message: love God with all your heart, mind, and soul. Love one another, even your enemies. Show compassion. Give back. Live selflessly. So simple. And for that He had to die. I asked so much from Him, but He asked so little of others. And people down here think that life is unfair. They don't know the half of it."

"But where do I come into the picture? I have no idea why you're telling me all this. After all, Moses and the prophets and your Son were all men. Why are you talking to me, a woman? Oh, I know, what Paul says about the fact that followers of your Son are neither Jew nor Greek, bond nor free, male or female, but the reality of the world of 2008 is that for a lot of people, women and outsiders, anyone who is different, along with the poor and disenfranchised have little or no power. We don't get the attention of the power brokers of the world, whether they are prophets or kings, so to speak. Even among some Christians, the right of women to have any voice in the church is a no-no."

"That's exactly why I'm talking to you right now. I'm looking down every day, that's day in your terms, not mine and I'm seeing this mess. The world is littered with trash, literal and metaphorical. Wars are killing my children everyday, that's MY children, you understand, not to mention the scourges of poverty, hunger, and disease that are rampant every which way I look.

"You humans look at the beautiful, pictures of a perfect planet taken by the crews of the space shuttles and the space station and you see Earth without all its blemishes. I see through the density of clouds, past the hues of blues and greens right down to every plant and tree, every creek, every bird and fish, every valley and mountain, every man, woman, and child. I see the destruction of forests and villages. I feel the pain of geese caught in oil spills and children orphaned by missile strikes. I understand the frustration of mothers caring for dying children and fathers unable to bring food to their families. It doesn't stop and I can't stop seeing and feeling because I have all the emotions, I share all the sorrows as well as the happiness of each of my children who reside on the most beautiful of all the worlds I have created. And just like every other human being in the world, I know what it means to grow frustrated by thinking of what could be instead of accepting what is. All I want is for human beings to go back to playing by my rules and living by applying them as my Son tried to show them, instead of making up their own as they go along for their own selfishness and show of power. It's that simple. That's where you come in."

"Me? How can it be me? I'm no Moses. I don't have any prophesying skills that I'm aware of. And how could I explain this to anyone? Who would believe me? People would think I had some kind of God complex or something. By the way, I need to be heading home. I don't know how long I've been gone . . ."

"Almost two hours."

"Two hours? And I didn't even tell Bob which direction I was heading. He'll be out looking for me, driving all over the place . . ."

"Not to worry. He's taking a nap. He won't miss you for another hour or so. By that time you'll be home."

"I think you have the wrong person. To put it very bluntly, I'm not good enough for this job."

"To put it even more bluntly, no one is. Look at all the ones who've disappointed me. Moses killed an Egyptian. David committed adultery and was an accomplice to murder. Jonah tried to run away from me and he lacked all compassion for the Ninevites. Peter denied my Son, Thomas doubted his resurrection. Even Paul, the first and greatest missionary of them all, could be the biggest pain in the neck you could imagine. And that doesn't begin to take in the history of the past two thousand years. There are days I'm not sure I can get off my throne—there's not really a throne at all, you know—and face another hundred years.

"What makes you expect to be different? You're human, aren't you? Every one of you is flawed. There I've said it. Somewhere along the line, I put in or left out a missing gene or something. You want to call it free will, which is fine with Me, but I know better.

"As for choosing you, I know I have the right person. And if you're not, I'll hand it off to someone else, just as I did in the old days. I'm going to give you the three best reasons why I've selected you for this job."

"Only three?"

"One. You are a woman. I've given this a lot of thought. All these years I've sent my message through men, which might not have been the right thing to do. After all, I do have my feminine side, you know, something else that most humans have a way of overlooking. Think about it. If I created both male and female and gave them distinct features and characteristics, wouldn't I have needed some prior knowledge of what each one would turn out to be? Where would that come from? As for giving men the say all this time, that probably came from the male's need to dominate, which I didn't take into consideration while I was going through the process. You must understand that the inventor of a thing that has never existed before must usually produce a large number of prototypes before the final model gets to the showroom.

"Are you telling me that God can make a mistake? How do I get that into the record without creating a maelstrom?"

"Not exactly mistakes in the way that humans think of mistakes. Let me give you an example. When I created the giraffe, I gave him a short neck, not taking into account that the trees in the Garden of Eden were extremely tall. Well, the poor thing had a hard time reaching up to get those leaves, so I gave him an extension. As I have intimated, Creation involved a lot of trial and error. But I know you can handle these very personal revelations with a great deal of discretion. You've kept a lot of secrets in your time."

"I have, I suppose, but I didn't realize You had secrets you were keeping."

"Think about that for a moment. Remember how Paul put it: 'Now I see through a glass darkly, but then face to face. Then I shall be known even as I am known.' Down through the ages, the whole idea of God has been a mystery and each religion, each generation, in every part of the world I've given you, has been trying to learn the mystery, thus to unravel the secrets that lead to The Ultimate Truth. The danger has been, and will forever be, those who believe that only they have that Truth, and try to force it on others who are weaker and more vulnerable. Verily, verily, I say unto you."

"Back to choosing me because I'm a woman. In whatever way You tell me to deliver your message, I'll be threatened, discredited, and maligned because of that physical attribute that You bestowed on me, along with the color of my eyes, my height, and yes, even my weight, which I'll admit is also of my own doing."

"The bottom line is this. Just like a coach, I've always gone with my starting lineup, but when they don't get the job done, for whatever reason, sooner or later, you have to send in the second string, not that I'm suggesting that as far as you're concerned. However, it's painfully clear that the first team, in this case, "men", aren't measuring up to their promise of fixing up the mess or, figuratively speaking, winning the game, so I'm giving you the chance. Believe it or not, like many of your sisters walking around on this earth, I'm just as tired of having old Eve blamed for all the evils of humankind as you are. That wasn't my intention in commissioning someone to write the story of Creation. Sure, I read the first draft, but I didn't take the story the way most of the readers and interpreters did. The whole business got out of hand. It's hard for me to accept the fact that people are still arguing over how, when, and how long Creation took. There are more important things to debate, such as how we get the human race to give up its power struggles, destruction of the environment, and the killing of fellow human beings."

"But . . ."

"That's reason number one. I'm choosing you because you are a woman, not in spite of it. Reason number two is that you can write with clarity and simplicity. I also know that your primary ambition as far as your writing is concerned is that you produce something of intrinsic value to your community, the society of which you are a part. You have ambition but not the kind that the world looks on with starry eyes and applause. I also know your head is full of ideas and you find yourself trying to figure out which one to tackle first and in doing so, you often come down with a terrible case of writer's block. Then you do produce something you believe has merit, send it off and the rejection that follows leads you back into the Valley of Despair but, and this is key, eventually you bounce back and give it another try. I once heard you tell a friend. 'I figure that if you keep throwing darts at the board, sooner or later you'll hit the bull's eye.' You've also asked me over and over to show you what I want you to do with your writing. Well, girl, this is it. What better way to get your attention than to just show up in the form of a flaming azalea and lay it on the line for you?"

"But . . ."

"Yeah, I know what you're thinking. You're not a theologian or a religious leader. You're not the pastor of a church or a TV evangelist. What you think you're missing is the language, the jargon of the "chosen ones, the ordained of God," from whatever denomination, sect, religion, or creed that's out there, trying to worm their way into the hearts, minds and pockets of those who don't or won't think for themselves. Forget all the terminology, the five syllable words, the original Hebrew and Greek words that mean whatever someone who wants to impress you tells you, the Q documents, the debates over eschatological nuance, the dates of the writings of the Gospels; in other words, the never ending story of trying to decipher the Bible, either in its entirety or book by book. To paraphrase a certain segment of society: It ain't going to happen! I know you hate that word, but here's another little secret. I don't give a rat's tail about correct grammar. If you listened to as many languages as I do in one second, you'd understand.

"Which brings me to you, my dear. You're smart but not too smart. You understand the basics: the Ten Commandments, the rules, so to speak. You are acquainted with Jesus and his message. You 'get' the finer points. You are also well read and inquisitive. You have people skills. You are able to connect the dots in terms of associating, let's say, the written word with people's actions. And you are here in this place right now, exactly where I showed up today because I happened to look down and saw this magnificent specimen of my creation and said to myself, I'm going to take a closer look at that. It's pretty good, even if I do say so myself. Sort of like a child who's painted a pleasing representation of a horse or a house or best friend. Then you showed up, along with the idea that I would speak to you, then waited to see what would transpire and here we are.

"Wait a minute. I didn't know You would speak to me. Did I?

"Don't you occasionally tell your friends and acquaintances that God speaks to you all the time as you're out and about taking in His creation?"

"Well, if You put it that way, I suppose so, but hearing You actually say the words does not seem real. So, exactly what am I supposed to do with these three outstanding, not to mention unique, qualifications?"

"Haven't figured it out yet, huh?"

"I have an inkling of an idea, but I'd rather hear it from you directly, as in The Lord said . . ."

"I want you to write the Ten Commandments for the twenty-first century complete with up to the minute terminology and illustrated with examples from real life that the average man, woman, and child can understand, regardless of social status, political affiliation, religious preference or educational background."

"Oh, my God!" I am caught off guard by the glibness of my tone.

"Well, you got that part right. As I've pointed out previously, I too have a sense of humor. No offense taken."

"And you're serious about this? This is You talking to me, just as you did with Moses and the burning bush."

"I'm always serious about my relationship with my creation, even if I do joke about it once in a while. This is your mission, Phyllis, should you decide to accept it, which I would if I were you. Don't try to run from it. You know what happened to Jonah."

I stare at the flaming azalea, looming high above me, my present day burning bush, as I question the reality of my physical body, my sanity and essence of my own humanness. I glance at my watch. Only twenty-five minutes have passed since I left my house, at least a mile over the nearest hill. I turn back. I have so many questions without answers.

"I'll be available any time you need me. The answers will come when you need me."

"How did You . . ." I can't believe He has chosen a person with such a limited understanding.

"Hey, you're just one of many. Human beings were to be the ultimate of Creation, the best of the best, so to speak. It's my problem, not yours. I'll work with what I've handed myself. You should be heading back. Bob will be waking up in about fifteen minutes and wondering where you are."

"Should I tell him about . . . well, meeting You here and what you want me to do?"

"I'd wait a while on that. In the meantime, don't worry about getting started or having the proper motivation. When you're ready, the ideas and the words that explain them will come to you. Not that you won't have to do some serious editing along the way, but I know how much you enjoy that part of writing!"

Did I actually hear God laughing at me at that moment, or was it only the wind happily rustling through the unfolding new leaves? Princess has finally made her way back to me and moves on but I am reluctant to follow her for the familiar path home has now become a vast unexplored territory.

How can so much happen in so little time? My feet refuse to move as I stand mesmerized by the brilliance of the overshadowing azalea. But as I gaze upward, I notice a fading of the flame-like colors, a dimming of their radiance as the reds and deep oranges become muted. The clouds are blocking the sunshine upon the petals, I think. But no, the sun is high overhead. I feel its warmth enclosing my body in a sauna cocoon.

God has spoken to me and moved on. Now I must turn back and choose a new way. I can accept the mission, but will I succeed? Will making the effort count for something? Will He tell me when I have completed the job or will I just know?

I didn't ask enough questions or even the right ones. I turn back to retrace my steps as I have not come far, but where is the flame azalea? It has faded from sight. Did I really see such a thing? Was that God's voice I heard or was I just making it up in my head, like writing a script for a play? There is only one way to find out. I have to study for the test that is to come. I must review material I have read and listened to since I was a child, the Ten Commandments, given to a disobedient, stubbornly sinful, wayward people that God refused to give up on. Nothing has changed, except the time and the place. He's still willing to give each one of us another chance, including me; therefore, I have no choice but to press on.

NOTE

I decided that the only way I can tackle this mission is to use my experience as both a high school English teacher and Sunday school teacher so as to treat each commandment as if it were a combination literature/Bible lesson that I would be presenting to any group of average young adults and older. My method is not intended to be patronizing or to minimize the importance of the Commandment. I am simply making a sincere effort based on my experience and understanding to explain the Commandments in every day terms and to give examples of how they are ignored or have been unconsciously abandoned through the influence of various forces in our society.

On the positive side, I hope to offer concrete examples of how the Commandments are respected, revered and adhered to by many members of whatever community we share, whether or not these fellow human beings identify themselves as Christians, Buddhists, Muslims, atheists, agnostics or through the use of other terms.

In the long run, I realize that I will end up being the one who learns the most from the lessons I try to teach. That's how it has always been and will continue to be for those who are called to teach and those who are willing to be taught.

COMMANDMENT NUMBER ONE:

THOU SHALT HAVE NO OTHER GODS BEFORE ME

In all probability, the major problem for most people in terms of understanding and therefore adhering to, or living by, the Ten Commandments, are the "thou shalts" and "thou shalt nots" of the King James Version of the Bible. Of course, those who are lovers of literature refer to its richness of language, *à la* Shakespeare, but as most any high school graduate remembers, for most students (and there are exceptions) the reading of the sonnets, *Julius Caesar, Hamlet, Macbeth* or any other of Will's great plays became the equivalent of being sent to Siberia to dig in the salt mines. I often used the aforementioned example to chastise my students for their tendency to complain about anything and everything. So, let us grant that the language is beautiful and mellifluous, although most of the major characters' actions center about lust, greed, ambition, adultery, murder and a host of other sins that could be summarize by one or more of the Ten Commandments.

The bottom line? Commandment Number One simply stated for the youngest of us through the oldest of us, with or without a graduate degree or money in the stock market boils down to this: If anything, and I emphasize the two parts of the word as in Any Thing, takes first place in your life other than

God, or what you understand or believe God to be, then you, we, all of us, are breaking the First Commandment.

Why is this the first commandment handed down to Moses for the spiritual welfare of his people, the hapless Hebrews wandering out and about, in and out of God's love and provision? According to every pastor, preacher, or teacher I've ever heard, along with the various commentaries I've read, this commandment is the foundation for all of our relationships here on earth, extending into our eternal life in heaven. The first five commandments give us the "rules" for accepting our roles as children of God, our Heavenly Father. If we acknowledge that relationship as first and foremost in life, then the rest is, proverbially, a piece of cake; although, of course, it has never been, nor will ever be, that simple.

Watch that baby learning to walk. The first step is the hardest. As human beings who come into this world with only a sense of the Me, with the demanding needs of Me always being of prime importance, acknowledging the existence of another being, a Greater Being, a Being Who Created this Me, is definitely beyond the intellectual capacity of us poor simpletons. In fact, I would guess that the higher the IQ, the greater this obstacle becomes.

Now suppose some of us do take that first step of accepting the idea of a God who is in fact the Creator of this Me, still the doubter, unable to comprehend the consequences of this tiny seed of faith. What comes next? Where does this business of "having no other gods before me" take me? What does it means in terms of my own thoughts and actions? Here is the struggle that each one of us faces on a daily basis. Why is it wrong to put anything or anyone before God? The question itself shows a lack of understanding of the seriousness of the commandment. The fact that we have come to use the word "wrong" as a euphemism for sin with such ease is an indication of our reluctance to deal honestly with the reality of sin in our lives.

Again I fall back on what I have been taught through the efforts of those devoted to spreading the Gospel and sharing their own faith, whether through sermons preached in a local church or the reading of helpful spirit-based messages, such as Rick Warren's *The Purpose Driven Life*, *The Road Less Traveled*, by M. Scott Peck, or John Killinger's *Bread for the Wilderness, Wine for the Journey*. The sum total of what I have learned in terms of why our relationship to God is of paramount importance goes back to Creation itself. God gave us human beings the precious gift of life, becoming in essence His "crown jewels" of Creation. We are here to bring honor and glory to His name, to sing His praises, to proclaim "the good news of His love" to the uttermost parts of this lovely planet that he designed as our home away from Home. If this spiritual understanding truly seeps into our very being, we would have no choice but to put God on the highest pedestal we can fathom, but we are a long way from that understanding and the powers of the material world that we share will stop at nothing to keep us from forging that unbreakable bond that ties us to God, our Creator.

Furthermore, we have read in Exodus 20:5 that our God is a jealous God, which seems like a strange concept to us. Why would an omniscient, omnipresent, omnipotent God have reason to be jealous of any other being or thing held up as a "god" by those who are simply unintentionally ignorant or those who willfully choose to deny the existence of any god or moral code as a means of preserving their place in the universe? The answer is right there under our noses. If our God is all He says He is and if we, even with our limited understanding, take Him at his word, why should He have to compete with any entity, real or imagined, concrete or abstract, animal, vegetable or mineral, without the power of one iota to confront the God of Creation?

Perhaps we can now attempt to deal with the second question that must be answered if we determine to accept, and thus adhere to, God's first commandment. Who and/or what are the "other gods" that we must not put before The God that we have come to know from the Old Testament or the Hebrew Bible?

The other gods are those we have created. They did not spring from our heads full grown, as Athena sprang from her father Zeus. No, they sprang from our imaginations and the imaginations of those whose influence surrounds us and envelops us with tantalizing tentacles of desire, tinted with the materialism that beckons us seductively to want, to need, to desire. We have created these gods in our own likeness—as in, what's there not to like? Sadly, we have taken the liking one step further: we have fallen in love with our gods. Think for a moment of how often we use the word love to describe our feelings for those things that can only be deemed as trivial. We *love* such and such a TV show; we *love* Kentucky Fried Chicken; we *love* the latest Faith Hill album; we *love* watching the World Series; we *love* shopping for shoes. You can replace any one or all of the above with your own choices, but the result is the same. The word *love* has been trivialized beyond our concept to use it to express the purest and deepest of all emotions.

This kind of "loving" inevitably takes us to the next step; that of idolizing that which we profess to love, especially in regard to persons well known to the public. How else to explain the phenomenon of frenzied fans awaiting the appearance of super stars such as Oprah, Jeff Gordon, Michael Jordan, Bruce Springsteen, along with such pseudo-celebrities as Paris Hilton, O. J. Simpson, and Vanna White. And then there are those with household names whose talents have not yet risen to the surface. I'll let you supply that list on your own. The end result is stadiums filled to capacity with adoring, shrieking fans paying outlandish sums of money to see the star athlete, the current No. 1 box office star, the hottest ticket on Broadway, whoever is on top, whatever is getting the most hits, all in the name of good, old-fashioned show biz, which for the most part is selling trash and soft porn to an adoring, unquestioning public. In terms of putting no other gods before our God, we should ask ourselves if we would bestow the same fervor and adoration if He suddenly showed up at the Hollywood Palace or the London Palladium. A simpler way of looking at this issue is to take a good, hard look at church attendance in countries that have a strong religious heritage and note the percentage of citizens who are faithful in attendance and in support of the mission of their local church, synagogue, or other place of worship.

Even among the faith community, putting God at the top of the agenda is often compromised by worldly concerns, such as making sure the service concludes in time for the Super Bowl, the NBA playoffs, the Indy 500, or whatever happens to be the major sporting event of the week. Dean Smith, former basketball coach at UNC–Chapel Hill, rose several more notches in my estimation of modern-day role models when he protested the idea that college basketball games would enter the Sunday night TV programming schedule. My limit on secularism creeping into the church came on a Wednesday night when a local steel drum band dedicated *Wasting Away in Margaritavile* to our assistant pastor!

Of course, there are plenty of other things that we deem from time to time or on a regular basis as more important than God or the requirements He has laid out for us as the stewards of his Creation. Look at the focus on money and what it can get for us: a fancy mega-mansion complete with killer mortgage, the fastest, spiffiest car on the market, even if it is a gas guzzler, $360

Gucci shoes, a $15,000 wedding, a cruise around South America, an iPhone or Blackberry to keep track of all the important names, dates and events in our busy lives, the latest technological gadget, the best HDTV, with no end in sight. We are consumed with consuming, working for our own self-gratification rather than laboring to forge a spiritual bond with our Creator that, in turn, will lead us to develop caring, compassionate, and loving relationships with our fellow travelers on this planet.

Perhaps this is what Jesus had in mind, as recorded in Luke 19, when the rich young man came to him asking what he should do to receive eternal life. Jesus told him to keep the commandments. "What commandments?" the young man asks and we cringe because we think smugly, "Well, everyone knows The Commandments, don't they?"

Obviously not, as Jesus goes through the list for him. "I have always obeyed all the commandments," he answers, pleased with himself, "What else do I have to do?" He is probably thinking that Jesus will pat him on the head and send him off to wait for the Second Coming, but not a chance. Jesus refuses to let him off so easily.

"Go and sell everything you have and give it to the poor. Then come and follow me." There it is. The young man, in coming to Jesus, had referred indirectly to Jesus as being good. Jesus reminded him that "only One is good." He is obviously pointing to God and asking the young man to make the connection. If he does so, realizing that Jesus is Lord, the embodiment of God, then his next step will be to put Jesus at the top of his priorities, forsaking all others in order to follow him.

The young man, we are told, is sad and walks away from Jesus because he will not give up his wealth. The love of money and what it can buy has first place in his life; thus it has become his god. He cannot follow Jesus and leave what my husband refers to as "stuff" behind. The ending of the story serves as a dramatic wake up call. Though we may not identify ourselves in terms of great wealth, we recognize ourselves in the young man's actions. We too have walked away because we could not give up something we mistakenly thought to be more important than following Him.

Recently I came across an anonymous quote in a devotional magazine that seems to explain the first commandment by answering the "Why?" of the child residing in each of us. We dare not put other Gods before Him, because "Whatever does not begin with God will end in failure." Taking that to its logical conclusion, it is obvious that all the ills of this present world can be traced back to our disobedience of God's first law.

ASSESSMENT

Take the time to make an honest assessment of your own relationship to God by taking an inventory of those things that you have made your personal gods, placing them before the one true God, the Creator and Sustainer of all life.

COMMANDMENT NUMBER TWO:

DON'T MAKE IDOLS OF ANYTHING THAT I HAVE CREATED

THE SECOND COMMANDMENT FOCUSES ON the creation of idols as representatives of the gods that He has forbidden us to place before him in the first commandment. We would do well to start by defining the terms, as champion debaters are taught. An "idol" according to one dictionary is "a representation or a symbol of a deity used as on object of worship." Another definition is "an object of passionate devotion." An idol, therefore, can be a person, place, or thing. An idol can be concrete or abstract. It can also be intangible as well as tangible. Think of the current mania for *American Idol* or the idolization of sports teams or designer fashions, in the forms of clothing, jewelry or perfume. Whatever is at the top of "the" List is what many of us want, aim for, and perhaps even desire, for a special birthday, anniversary, or Christmas gift, the irony of ironies.

It might be useful to define other words that are linked to that of idol. For instance, an idolater is, obviously, "a worshiper of idols," or "a person who admires or loves intensely and often blindly." Idolatry is defined as "the worship of a physical object as a god," or "an immoderate attachment or devotion to something." To idolize is "to love or to admire to excess." Whether concentrating on one form of the word and its definition or putting them altogether, there is no doubt that our modern society is part and parcel of the very conspicuous institution of idolatry. In fact, it would be hard to offer up any part of American life, whether in business, education, media, politics, advertising, or even religion itself, that has not been undermined or contaminated by the insidious practice of idolatry of those caught in its web.

We often refer to people we admire as our idols. We "idolize" positions to which we aspire or places we want to visit, along with particular purchases that loom in the future as material aspirations. Sports at all levels use mascots as idols to root for and to emulate by buying every manner of conceivable paraphernalia that bears the desired logo or caricature. A conservative inventory of the idols represented in a typical American home would truly be mind-boggling. Add to that the amount of money spent in our country in trivial idol pursuit by not only adults but by our children as well and it becomes crystal clear that the good ol' USA has probably never met an idol it did not take to its bosom in one form or another.

God specifically details the objects of his creation that "form anything in heaven above," such as the sun, moon, stars, and comets. Then he moves to "the earth beneath," which obviously includes trees, animals, mountains, and birds. Finally, He restricts the worship of anything "in the waters below." Whales, fish of any kind, seals, sea lions, starfish, and dolphins come to mind. Of the universe He has created, nothing is omitted. With three broad sweeps he has taken every entity that we humans might be tempted to elevate to god status off the table.

Interestingly, we know that many cultures throughout history have worshiped many of these entities as they tried to establish a relationship to a higher power through nature. Consider the Maya Indians and their worship of the jaguar or the Greeks and Romans with their multitude of gods that focused on both the known world, such as the sun and the sea, along with intangible attributes of mankind, such as wisdom and love. In their effort to cover all the basics the Greeks, according to Paul in Acts 17:23, had constructed an altar with the inscription: To An Unknown God. Paul seized the opportunity to explain to the Athenians that what they worshipped as unknown was God, the Lord of everything in heaven and earth. He goes on to instruct the his audience in verses 29–30, to not think of this divine being in terms of silver, gold, or stone; in other words, not an image of anything that can be made by man. Furthermore, he explains to his listeners, there was a period when God could overlook such ignorance, but the time has arrived when God "commands" every person to repent. He then refers indirectly to Jesus and his resurrection. Clearly Paul, an educated Jew who knew the Commandments from his childhood, is tracing the "good news" back to the foundation of God and His supreme authority to provide His creation with the rules for living.

At the same time, we are made aware that God knew that human beings with their limited understanding would create deities based on their environments and experiences. In the end, however, the worship of these objects would only take them farther from the One for whom they searched.

In His instructions to Moses, God provides the rationale for this second commandment in basic parental language. If you don't follow this commandment, your children and their children will suffer because He will punish them for their worship of any idol, no matter what form it may take. He doesn't mince words here, telling the children of Israel through his spokesman, Moses, that putting other gods before Him, no matter what form they may take, is the equivalent of hating God. It would seem that most of us have been guilty of selective hearing when we come to the detailed explanations found in Exodus 20:5.

The inescapable conclusion as Isaiah reminded us is that "like sheep, we have all gone astray" and we keep on going astray because we aren't following the Lord, our Shepherd. We have to do it our way, as I've heard from so many teenagers, even if we make mistakes. I imagine that's how Moses thought of his people, as silly immature adolescents, when he came down from the mountain after spending all that time with God, only to find "the chosen ones" drinking and carrying on with their new god, the golden calf. Moses was up there taking notes just as fast as he could to get it right for his people and they were breaking the rules faster than God could hand them out. As a wise man once pointed out, "There's nothing new under the sun."

On the other hand, like any good and wise parent, God doesn't give up on us. He provides the most valuable incentive of all for his good and faithful servants, that of continuously showing His love in return for those who love Him and keep His commandments even, as Exodus 20:6 informs us, unto a thousand generations. If I am correct, twenty years is deemed a generation. That adds up to 20,000 years of unending love to those who follow the commandments and teach their children to do likewise!

Ah, we might be tempted to exclaim, if the history of the Hebrews covers some six thousand years plus, we still have perhaps thirteen thousand or more years to reap God's unending love! We have failed to take into account, that for all the goodness that has existed and does presently exist in our present time, we can not put ourselves into the mind of God and weigh the percentages of those who love Him and keep his commandments and those who don't.

How do the scales look from God's vantage point? I dare

think that not one on us would be willing to wager one thin dime on the most important question facing us today. Though I cannot begin to comprehend the magnitude of God as an Intelligent Being, my own limited intelligence tells me that He is deeply disappointed with us, and like any loving parent, He keeps on loving us; but that doesn't mean He isn't angry as He observes us downgrading His status while we elevate our favorite basketball, football or baseball teams and their star players to the top places on the MVP list of our real priorities.

ASSESSMENT

Visualize specific examples of modern "idols" to which you have devoted time, energy, talents and money, rather than serving the God who demands your utmost love and devotion.

COMMANDMENT NUMBER THREE:

DO NOT MISUSE THE NAME OF THE LORD YOUR GOD

How many times a day do we hear such expressions as "Oh, my God," "Dear Lord," "Lord Almighty," "Good God," and other variations that come to mind, all without any semblance of religious or spiritual context? In our homes, our offices, in public places, such as theatres, restaurants, shopping malls, airport terminal waiting rooms, the air is rife with the use of God's name for reasons that are both mundane and profane. In fact, as I learned early in my high school teaching career, most young people are completely unaware that there is anything wrong with such usages. "You are taking the Lord's name in vain," I would attempt to inform, using the King James Version of the Third Commandment.

"So, what does that mean, anyway?" someone might persist, while in the back another brave, or slightly arrogant, soul proclaims, "This ain't church. You can't teach nothing about the Bible to us," unaware that she had fallen into my deadly trap of "This is my classroom. Any language that offends anyone in this class is off limits. There are people in this class who believe in God, in whatever way they may choose, including your teacher, and this speech offends us, so it won't be allowed."

"OK, we get that, but now that you've got that off your

chest, do you mind explaining to us why it's the wrong thing to do?" The tone has softened a bit. There is a definite leaning towards the teacher; others are listening carefully. This is a teachable moment involving good grammar, good manners, a little bit of culture, and a little bit of literature. I'm not selling any particular brand of religion or Christianity. I'm just answering the question, as in "inquiring minds want to know."

Most people don't "get" this commandment because it is so blatantly broken in our society. In fact, we probably are subject to these irreverent references to God so frequently that we probably don't hear them; and if we do, they rarely cause offense on our part. Rather, we are most likely to pretend not to notice as a means of avoiding confrontation or hurting someone's feelings, especially if that someone is a friend or member of our family. The point is that we have allowed a person to hurt God's feelings and not spoken up on His behalf. We have put aside our spiritual integrity.

I would argue that parents, pastors, and teachers who repeatedly point out the misuse of the Lord's name and give the reasons why such usage is inappropriate and harmful are performing a great service, not only for their children, but for society as well.

To go back to one of my answers to my own students as to why we "shouldn't" speak God's name lightly, I would remind them of the story of "The Boy Who Cried Wolf."

After reviewing the basic plot of the story, I ask, "Do you remember the moral of that story?"

"Sure," some one answers. "He cried 'wolf' so many times just to get attention that when the wolf finally appeared and he was really crying for help, no one answered."

"Right. Now here's the point. Have you ever prayed for something important, such as a friend getting well or getting a good grade, after you've studied, of course, on a hard test?"

Ninety-nine percent of hands usually fly into the air.

"And do you start your prayers with words such as such as 'Dear God, or Heavenly Father, or Lord God?"

Nods of affirmation follow.

"So you're expecting God to hear your prayers, right?"

"Of course!" they chorus enthusiastically.

"But what if you've been fooling around, just calling His name in a disrespectful way whenever it crosses your mind, not even thinking about what it means? Calling His name, whatever the form, has nothing to do with thanking God or praising His name, or asking Him for his help. It's just 'God' this, and 'Oh, Lord' that, and even a few 'Goddamns' thrown in for good measure, which incidentally means that you are asking God to condemn someone or something to hell. (For the record, I have found that this particular information makes a very deep impression of most young people.) You think God is paying attention to that kind of talk from you?"

The silence is palpable. Finally, a young man answers, "He's always listening, isn't he?"

The others follow suit. "He hears everything."

Someone laughs, "Just like Santa Claus!"

Another voice, "Hey, man, this is serious sh—, uh, stuff, we're talking about. Right?"

"Right." They are with me now. They are thinking hard about the conversation that has been taking place.

"How come nobody ever explained it to us?" a girl asks.

"How come everybody does it, even on TV and in the movies, you know? How can so many people be getting this wrong?"

I wonder the same thing. I wonder why we let this talk come into our living rooms and dens. I wonder why we let our children listen to those who constantly talk trash of any kind, including misusing the Lord's name. I wonder why we laugh at TV characters, who constantly say, "Oh, my God," as an afterthought to every spilled cup of coffee, every relationship gone bad, every soiled diaper, every lost purse, and every curvy blonde that walks into a gala affair.

One thoughtful young woman raises her hand. I know her parents are Christian, and she is a faithful churchgoer. "Is that why the King James Bible tells us not to take the Lord's name in vain? That if we call his name without really thinking about who He is or what we're doing, it will come to nothing, because we're not taking Him seriously, we're not giving Him the respect He deserves?"

Others in the class are watching her and listening intently. One by one they nod in affirmation. The mood is very solemn. I feel like I'm in Sunday school. If these young people can grasp such a simple concept, why don't adults, I ask myself.

"There is one additional part of the commandment that I haven't brought to your attention. After Moses gives the people of Israel this commandment, he follows with the admonition, which means warning, that God will not hold anyone guiltless who misuses His name. Simply put, he is telling the people that those who break this rule are going to be punished. It's the same thing as if you break a rule here in school, whether it's in the lunchroom or in my classroom. There are always consequences for those who choose to disobey."

The solemn atmosphere is broken by the class clown, who quips, "You better watch out, Mrs. Stump, before someone sues you for preaching instead of teaching."

Everyone laughs. Then another voice speaks up, "Ain't nobody gonna sue Mrs. Stump! She be teaching us how to speak the right words for the right reason!" The class explodes in another round of laughter and I join in.

Now back to square one. The Bible beginning in the Old Testament, or Hebrew Bible, and continuing through the New Testament reiterates the Third Commandment. Isaiah 57:15 reminds us of the law of the "high and lofty One . . . whose name is holy." The definitions of the word "holy" provide more than ample reasons for the awe that should accompany any use of God's name. They include: "characterized by perfection and transcendence: commanding absolute adoration and reverence."

Joel 2:32 tells us that those who call on His name will be saved, reinforcing the power of God's name. In Zechariah 12:9, the prophet reveals that when the day of the Lord comes, "there will be one Lord, and his name the only name." Nothing else, no one else will have any value, any importance, or any claim on our loyalty or allegiance. Now is the time to start cleaning out the closets of those idols that are cluttering up our empty lives.

Then we come to the New Testament and the birth of Christ. Early in his ministry, Jesus models for his disciples in Matthew 6:9-10 the way his followers should pray. In addressing God as "Our Father," Jesus is giving us a new idea of the relationship that we should have with the One who has created us. He continues by saying, "Hallowed be your name." Those of us who have prayed these words for a lifetime may have uttered them without understanding the depth of their meaning. The word *hallowed* is related to the word "holy," which we have previously explored. Definitions include: as a verb, "to make holy or set apart for holy use"; "to respect greatly." Used as an adjective, as in the prayer of Jesus, it means "consecrated," "sacred."

The disciples were Jews, faithful and knowledgeable of the laws and the commandments. They were aware of their history as God's chosen people. Surely they understood the sacredness and reverence due to the One True God who had led their ancestors out of bondage in order to make the journey that would take them to His Son, but Jesus makes sure that they do not forget that God's name should always be elevated and set apart.

The coming of Jesus presents another dilemma for both Christian and non-Christian in the matter of "name calling," because the One who is God's representative on earth has become part of the Holy God as one member of the Trinity. In Matthew 18:19, Jesus tells his disciples that whatever they ask of God when they gather in His name will be done, leaving no doubt that the name Jesus is synonymous with other names directed to the One True God. Yet, sadly, how often is Jesus's name misused, even by those who verbally doubt His existence, not to mention His lordship.

One prominent comedian once quipped, with a resulting roar of laughter from his audience, that he was twelve years old before he realized that his name wasn't Jesus Christ, as it was the only response he ever provoked from his father. Everywhere we turn, it's "Jesus!" or "Jesus Christ!" from anything to the car breaking down, to an overcharge on a late bill, to a spilled entrée in someone's lap, to missing a plane. The utterances are, however, not prayers of penitence or petition. Instead, they are blasphemous words that demean the single most important human being who ever walked this earth. Jesus Christ.

ASSESSMENT

PART 1. Select one day and monitor the number of times you hear the names of God and Jesus spoken in ways that do not suggest adoration, respect or honest petition. This includes overheard conversations, TV programs, song lyrics, and movie dialogue. You might want to check out reading materials as well.

After making your count, are you surprised at the number of incidents you encountered or observed? Were there more or fewer incidents than you expected?

PART 2: (This may be the harder assignment for you.) Ask family, friends and coworkers to monitor your own speech for one day. Ask them to stop you if you use any term referring to God or Jesus in a way that is not related to prayer or petition. Keep a running total from the time you get up until you go to bed.

PART 3: Determine a course of action in situations where this language occurs. Keep in mind the relationship you may or may not have with the offenders. Do the same for yourself. What can you do to eliminate misusing the name of God or Jesus? Give yourself a penalty that can be used in a positive way, such as a monetary amount that will go to a specific cause: a mission project or a donation to a favorite charity.

If we are striving to follow God's laws and be His witnesses, we can overcome our weaknesses with prayer, Bible study and a plan of action. One suggestion is to read the Ten Commandments at some point each day and make a commitment to concentrate on upholding one commandment each day. Place a copy of the Commandments in a conspicuous place in your home or place of business. (If they are part of your designated workspace, no legal issues are at stake.) One caution is not to let yourself be caught up in a holier-than-thou attitude that sends a wrong message to those with whom you work or fellowship. Be sincere in your quest to "keep the commandments," but be humble about it. Your goal is to put the commandments to use to benefit your spiritual life; it is not to beat others over the head with them.

COMMANDMENT NUMBER FOUR:

REMEMBER THE SABBATH DAY TO KEEP IT HOLY

IN THE HANDING OUT OF the Fourth Commandment, God wastes no time in following it up with Commandment Four B: you will work for six days and do all your work. Then he lays down the law with unrelenting clarity beginning with the meaning of the Sabbath, which is, the seventh day. Next, God specifies the amount of work allowed: not any. Who is not allowed to work? Answer: Neither son nor daughter, servants—both male and female—cattle, or strangers (guests) who might be visiting for a while.

The rule and its definition of terms are not, however, the end of God's pronouncement. He proceeds to explain the rationale behind this particular law. The Lord, he tells us, referring to himself in the third person, completed creation, the heavens, the earth, the seas, and everything else that was a part of them, and then rested on the seventh day, which He then blessed and made holy. I understand this as God's sharing a very personal part of Who He is and What He about with his people.

Look here, I can hear him saying, *I did all this work. I didn't stop until it was finished, but when it was, I rested because I deserved it. I needed time to sit and contemplate what I had done. To be honest with you, I exceeded my own expectations and after those long, difficult six days, I was worn out and exhausted. My brain was almost on empty, my fingers worn to the nubs. Who doesn't need to sit a spell after such effort? Even God, I can tell you. And that's the point. When I put you in charge of everything on earth, I knew you'd have to work hard to make a go of it, and that some of you would go overboard, never wanting to stop for anything, even a cup of coffee or a glass of water. You'd wear yourself out before your allotted time was up. You'd drive your family and friends, along with anybody else who happened to be working for you, crazy with your mania for trying to get ahead. So, I decided to have you put aside one day, just one day out of seven, to rest, take a break, get yourself and your family, your work crews, even your friends and relatives, ready to start the new week with a renewed mind and a revived body. That's it, pretty simple, huh? Get your wife, or husband, to cross stitch it and hang it by the mirror in the bathroom so you can read it while you're combing your hair: THE SEVENTH DAY IS A HOLY DAY. NO WORK. JUST TAKE IT EASY.*

Fast forward to the year 2008. The Sabbath, whether it is the actual seventh day as practiced by Seventh Day Adventists or the Jewish community or Sunday, as practiced by Christians who view it as sacred because it was the day that Christ arose from the dead, has lost most of its flavor of holiness. To give credit where credit is due, it is highly probable that the two groups mentioned above do a better job of observing the true spirit of the Sabbath than those of us who are regular Sunday-go-to-church Christians.

The first couple of hours, after getting up and getting dressed, are pretty easy. We head off to Sunday school for Bible study, followed by a service of music, scripture and preaching, then head back home for an afternoon of shopping, watching football or basketball, going to a movie, visiting friends, or just doing nothing.

We may also wash a few loads of clothing, mow the yard,

wash the car, or paint the house. In most families, the members spread out after a quick lunch at some fast food restaurant, each one doing his or her own thing. Little kids play baseball or ride their bicycles in the neighborhood. Teenagers ride around town or head to the mall. Moms read novels or magazines, give themselves a manicure, maybe go for a walk. Dad sprawls out on the sofa, watches a game or two, and then settles down for a nap.

Somewhere nearby, people in a rest home wait for somebody to go and visit. Women in a shelter for victims of domestic violence wonder if they will ever be able to return to their homes without being afraid. At Walmart, shoppers are in a hurry, shouting at their children, and wondering if they have enough money to buy new outfits for their school age children. At restaurants, wait persons run from table to table, hoping to earn enough tips to get them through the next week. Large cities and small are flooded with cars here, there and everywhere, horns beeping, radios blaring, exhaust fumes filling the air with another large dose of greenhouse gases.

What does all this have to do with keeping the Sabbath holy? The big picture suggests it's pretty hard to work the line between the spiritual world that we yearn for and the material world that has captured us. All of us, no matter how devout or well-meaning, have succumbed to the ease with which the world intrudes on our intention to set aside the seventh day and make it a day of rest. Look at us as a collective people. We are overmedicated, overfed, and over stimulated, while at the same time, we are sleep deprived, credit card poor, and undernurtured in our spiritual lives.

Take a hard look at the businesses that serve us; twenty-four-hour fast food restaurants, service stations, and grocery stores; department stores that open at four and five A.M. the day after Thanksgiving; TV channels that run twenty-four hours a day. It makes me wonder if anybody is getting any sleep that's truly restful. As for putting aside all work for a whole day, forget it! Who could do that? Furthermore, some would ask, who would want to? And what's work, anyway? Isn't work, like beauty, in the eyes of the beholder? If I want to call putting the roof on the house play, can't I?

Well, of course. Which is how the Hebrews got caught up in all those laws and subdivisions of laws that led them down the path of losing their common sense to the extent that dragging a wounded ox out of a ditch would not be tolerated because that would be work! Today the pendulum has swung the other way. We no longer differentiate between the two activities to any great degree. Work is play, as in doing the yard work, fixing the car, or plowing the field to start a vegetable garden. It's rest, it's relaxation, it's good therapy, we say. Then there is play, as in all forms of professional sports, such as chasing a tiny ball all over acres of unnaturally green grass, or running high-speed cars round and round billion dollar racetracks, hoping all the while that there will be a thrilling accident, although we don't want anyone to be hurt or wind up in a hospital with a broken neck.

Of course, we're all guilty of taking a day that should be holy and making it in our image, instead of in God's. If I didn't choose to go out for lunch on Sunday, people wouldn't have to work in that restaurant. If I didn't go to the grocery, it wouldn't have to stay open and the people who work there could have a day of rest. If we took this attitude as far as it would go, I suppose the churches would be closed on Sunday, so the preacher wouldn't have to deliver a sermon and the music director wouldn't need to direct the choir so the organist wouldn't be required to play, because, after all, isn't what they do work, even if it's done in church ?

Forty or fifty years ago, the Fourth Commandment was in

a sense bolstered by Blue Laws in many places in this country. I'm sure many of us can remember the days when grocery stores and department stores, even gas stations, were closed on Sunday. Some of us also remember not being allowed to go to movies on Sunday or play cards or watch television. People in small towns didn't wash cars or mow laws on Sunday. It was understood that that was how it was and would be world without end. Amen.

But slowly, things began to change. The adage, the Sabbath was made for man, not man for the Sabbath, which is Biblical, began to be bandied about as a rationale for being able to do whatever pleased us, whether it was foregoing church services to go fishing or finishing our last minute Christmas shopping. It's not for any one, except God, to say how or what we should do with our time on Sundays, or the Sabbath, whichever we observe. I'm guessing that most of us break the commandment, whether in great ways or in small. I've set my own rules, which may not amount to anything that affects the intent of the law one way or the other. I don't wash clothes or use the dryer. Do I use the dishwasher? I don't think so. The problem with me is the noise. I don't think noise helps us keep the day holy.

Do I listen to music or watch TV? Yes, but I monitor what I listen to or watch; eliminating content that may be violent, blatantly sexual, or profane as far as actions or language. (See how easy it is to rationalize?) In fact, my husband and I have basically quit watching TV because we find most of it to be "garbage," our term of disapproval. Even commercials can be disgusting or distasteful. I don't like to shop on Sunday, although occasionally, I may run to the drugstore or grocery store, if I find myself without something I really need. Thus I end up breaking my own rules as well as the Sabbath, but I do try to make Sunday a quiet day, a day of rest and contemplation. I take walks, check out my gardens, maybe pick a bouquet of flowers, sit down and write notes to friends, watch *All Creatures Great and Small*, fix a simple lunch, read magazines or a book with some meat to it, not the "fluff" that passes for good writing.

Am I keeping the Fourth Commandment? Am I trying to be aware of my choices as I spend each Sunday, first at church, then in my home? I want to honor all of God's commandments. Some seem harder than others, to be sure. The bottom line is that we take this day, the seventh day, the Sabbath, for granted. God didn't. He had done a wondrous work. He needed the rest.

ASSESSMENT

How do you spend your Sundays, or seventh days? Is the worship of God for His great work of Creation part of your regular routine? Take the time to evaluate how you spend your time on Sunday and how you relate to the Fourth Commandment. Make a list of Do's and Don'ts for your own observance of the Seventh Day. Ask yourself if a true day of rest would be beneficial to you. If your answer is Yes, then make a plan of how you can make it happen for you and others in your family.

COMMANDMENT NUMBER FIVE:

ALWAYS GIVE HONOR TO YOUR MOTHER AND FATHER

WITH COMMANDMENT NUMBER FIVE, God moves us into the area of human relationships, beginning with the most obvious: the relationship with our parents. For many of us, this commandment involves the hardest work and the most difficult questions we must face concerning our own existence. In all probability, each person contemplating the meaning of this commandment, along with the task of carrying out its intended purpose, will fall into one of three categories:

CATEGORY NO. 1: My parents are the greatest in the world. Sure they've made mistakes, but they've been there for me all the way. They've been supportive; they've tended to my needs; and they've provided me with strong moral and spiritual values. I couldn't have asked for better parents and I'm eternally grateful for all they've done for me.

To take this one step further, from your own perspective, what percentage of people who might be asked how they would rate their parents, would give the above answer? (I personally have no statistics and am wondering myself.)

CATEGORY NO. 2: My dad, or my mother, is a wonderful person. I adore him. I owe everything I am to her. On the other hand, my mother, or my dad, hasn't really been the parent I could look up to. He has had other problems that have kept our family off balance and my mother has had to carry ninety percent of the weight of raising me the right way. She put too much emphasis on work; he had a problem with alcohol, or drugs, or being involved with other people. I don't dislike my mom, or my dad, but I lost respect for him a long time ago. I'm not bitter about it. That's the way life is for some of us.

As in CATEGORY NO. 1, what percentage of those asked how they rate their parents would put themselves in CATEGORY NO. 2?

CATEGORY NO. 3: Don't talk to me about my parents! Both of them were so messed up, and they took us kids down with them. Because of them, I ended up . . . being placed in foster care, in a group home, being raised by my grandmother, in jail, pregnant, dropping out of school. (Choose any that apply.) How am I supposed to show respect to people who not only showed no respect for their children, (Want to see the bruises? Some of them you can't see), but had no respect for themselves? They may be parents in the biological sense but in the sense of being real parents, forget it. From where I am right now, I think any male person can plant a seed for a baby and any female person can go through the whole birthing process, but that doesn't make either one of them a parent. If God wanted me to honor my parents, He could have at least given me some decent ones who deserved the honor.

What percentage do you think of those asked concerning their relationships with their parents would put themselves in CATEGORY NO.3?

How did I come up with these categories? I heard variations of all three categories from teenagers in four different schools in my thirty-year teaching career. I myself fit into Category No. 2 due to the fact that my alcoholic biological father abandoned my mother and me when I was three. At age seven, my mother remarried and my stepfather turned out to be an alcoholic and also a child molester, thus causing me to sometimes identify myself as a CATEGORY 3 because I thought my mother could have done better by herself and me. I give her credit, however, for teaching me to love to read and encouraging me to always do my best. Those were in the early years when we were by ourselves. After my stepfather entered the picture, she pretty much left me to make it on my own, while giving me the additional burden of being her combination housekeeper-baby sitter when my two little sisters came along.

As Tom Hanks put it so aptly in *Apollo 13*, "We seem to have a problem," when it comes to living out the ideals of the Fifth Commandment. God has set the bar very high in admonishing us to honor our parents. He even holds out a little carrot as an incentive for us to follow the rule: "so that you may live long in the land I, as in the Lord your God, am giving you," as noted in Exodus 20:12b.

"But isn't He talking to the Hebrews?" we venture to suggest. "In fact, aren't the other Commandments directed to the Hebrews? And Moses is the mediator, right? Aren't we, therefore, off the hook because we're not the Hebrews? We live in another country. We have lots of different identities. How did we get caught up in this web of Commandments from so far back in history, with another culture, anyway?"

The arguments sound logical and reasonable. Maybe that's why so many of us aren't paying attention to these "old" commandments. We've made ourselves believe that they don't apply to us, at this time, in this country, in these circumstances where we call ourselves by many names that seem to be religious; Buddhist, Christian, Muslim, Hindu, with subdivisions of every mix imaginable. But, hold on a minute, if this argument holds any water at all, why have there been lawsuits over the placement of the Ten Commandments in courtrooms and other public places?

Suffice it to state for the premise of this discussion, that the Ten Commandments and variations thereof have been part of many cultures and religions for thousands of years. Jews and Christians fall back on the book of Exodus as the "textbook for the rules." Furthermore, Jesus refers to the Commandments throughout his ministry, even to the point of condensing them into Two Unequivocal Rules, which are found in Matthew 22:37-40. "Love the Lord God with all your heart and with all your soul and with all your mind. This is the first and greatest commandment." In effect Jesus is condensing Commandments Number One through Four into this one statement that so many Christians know by heart.

Then he continues, "And the second is like it; love your neighbor as yourself." This is Jesus summarizing the remaining six commandments, beginning with the idea of honoring, thus showing respect to our parents, who are essentially the first of the many "neighbors" who will play important roles in our lives. His final statement closes the case for obeying the commandments. "All the Law (the rules for our behavior here on this earth) and the Prophets (those who were singled out to teach and explain them to us clearly and effectively) hang (rest, have a foundation) on these two commandments." In other words, "That's it," Jesus states emphatically, "in a nutshell.

Still we face the age-old dilemma that has haunted our dreams, stymied our psychologists, social workers, ministers, teachers, and psychiatrists. How do we translate the anger, hatred, animosity, and perhaps even the feigned indifference held so deeply within us towards those who have done us great damage by not being the parents so lovingly and respectfully described in Category One?

Our only recourse is to understand that God knows. He knows the failings of those who were our mothers and fathers. He knows that they were imperfect human beings, as we ourselves are imperfect. He knows the hurts, the disappointments, the cries of pain, and the tears of self-pity that we have shed. He will not let us off the hook, however. If we are to expect forgiveness from Him, we can no less than forgive those who have done us great harm, starting with our parents.

It is noteworthy that God's commandment does not ask us to love, only to honor, or respect. Jesus adds the imperative that we must love because his birth, death and resurrection do not occur as a result of God's respect for us, his highest creation turned into wayward children. No, God's gift of His Son comes without strings, without a quid pro quo. "I do this for you," He tells us, "not because you deserve anything, but because I still love you, in spite of your miserable failings."

Commandment Number Five is the beginning of our journey to the place of unconditional love. It must start with our parents, no matter how tortuous the demands on our emotions, as well as our ability to reason. Perhaps God is asking us to read between the lines. "Honor your biological parents and respect them because they are the instruments that I have used to give you life. Without them, no matter how despicable or piteous they may have been in your sight, you would not have life. You would not exist. It is with these two imperfect human beings that you must start if you will ever learn to love your neighbors as yourself." I've been there and done that. Giving out the rules is the easy part. Teaching students to adhere to them takes every bit of knowledge, skill, creativity and nuance, not to mention physical exertion that one can muster up. The job never ends. The rewards are often intangible.

This great enlightenment opens another door of revelation. To love my neighbor means I must first love myself, but the sad truth is that I have not loved myself because of all the things I am or am not due to the failings of my parents. I am a bundled mess of distortion and dis-ease in the sense of the spiritual because of my undecipherable behaviors that I have visited upon myself and others due "to the sins of the fathers (and the mothers) unto the second and third generations." If we do not forgive, we cannot show respect. If we do not first have respect, we cannot move on to the next step: we will not learn to love.

If our days are to be long upon this earth, regardless of the actual term in years, God puts the rules right up there in the front of the room for all to see. "Follow the rules, He explains to us, "and all will go well. There won't be any problems in this place."

Alas. I've been there and done that. For thirty years, I posted the rules, explained them to my students on the first day or classes and promised them easy sailing if they would just pay attention to the Laws of My Classroom. Sorry to say, many broke the rules, some inadvertently, others clearly with a purpose in mind. I cannot pretend to understand the all-powerful God and His all-knowing Mind, but in many ways I can remind younger educators, we're not in this for the short-term. Something tells me that neither is God.

ASSESSMENT

Take a few minutes to write down an evaluation of your parents. List their positive attributes, the things that you admire (admired) about them, as well as the negatives that you may feel have harmed you. Do you feel that you have forgiven them for any harm done to you that has been the result of their behaviors? Do you feel a need to express forgiveness in some way, even if they are no longer alive? Have you come to a place in your heart that you can express respect for them, if for no other reason than that they gave you life? If you cannot answer the above questions in a positive way, can you think of a course of action that might help you get to the place of forgiveness? Do you have resources such as a best friend, minister, teacher or counselor that you would trust to help you work through these negatives in your life? The important thing is to take the first step in resolving the issue of how you can begin to honor your parents in order to move on to healthier relationships with others.

COMMANDMENT NUMBER SIX:

DON'T COMMIT MURDER

W*EBSTER'S DICTIONARY* DEFINES *MURDER*, the noun, as "the crime of unlawfully killing a person, especially with malice aforethought." The thought of murdering someone is unimaginable to most of us, yet the next thing we know, we're yelling "Kill the umpire!" at the baseball game or telling a spouse or child, "If you do that one more time, I'm going to kill you!" Of course, these are just figures of speech. After all, isn't it better to scream out your anger with words than actually taking an axe to that sorry excuse for a human being? People don't really take such language seriously. Or do they? Most of the time, we're just kidding. Aren't we?

Probably, but actions begin with words and words come from thoughts and . . . well, next thing we know we are in a heap of trouble, because somewhere deep inside, we are harboring just a little bit of malice, another word that calls for a definition. Back to Webster, which informs us that malice means ill will or more specifically, "the intent to commit an unlawful act or cause harm without legal justification or excuse."

The Sixth Commandment comes right to the point as it lays down, according to my husband's 1956 edition of *The New Bible Commentary*, edited by Francis Davidson, "a general safeguard of the sanctity of human life." Specific kinds of murder are dealt with in subsequent scriptures, such as excusable homicide in Exodus 21:13. Numbers 35:23 refers to accidental homicide, and a third example—justifiable homicide—is found in Numbers 22:2. It is easy to see the laws regarding murder in our modern day society evolving from the ancient laws based on "the ten words" that God imparted to Moses to deliver to His people as he came down from Mt. Sinai.

If we read further into the twenty-first chapter of Exodus, we are given a list of specific crimes that demand the death penalty, and the list continues through chapter twenty-two. In fact, Exodus 21:23–24, contains the words that are most used to support the death penalty in our country: "But if there is serious injury, you are to take life for life, eye for eye, tooth for tooth, hand for hand, foot for foot." Adhering to such a law, as one wise man has observed, will eventually create a generation of blind, toothless people who can neither walk nor work.

Though the Sixth Commandment consists of only four words, it would be simple to conjecture that it has been responsible for more laws designed to break down and explain the myriad nuances of the term, further causing more confusion, inequality, as well as debate, in delineating the crime and its punishment than any other in our country's history.

If, however, we are able to view the commandments as an inverted pyramid structure, we are able to see the grand design that God has given to humankind in these very important ten words. All law rests on the premise that God is the "I Am" of creation; He alone is to be worshipped. Each succeeding Commandment expands on that one idea as it takes us to the next level. By the time we reach Commandment Number Five, honoring our parents, we have moved from the worship of God to the relationships that we as human beings have with one another. We are God's creation. If we worship Him, we will revere the life that He has created, from our biological family to our neighbors all over the world, who are in the truest sense our extended family. The sanctity of life must be preserved. Although that is God's ideal and we as humans have found the ways and means to dilute the ideal, using terms such as justifiable, accidental, excusable, and the less condemnatory "manslaughter," the taking of any life destroys that which God has created for His own glory.

What about self-defense? May I, as in do I have permission, take someone else's life in order to preserve my own? That question came up many times over my thirty years of teaching high school English. I am very anti-gun and have always been, ever since the night my stepfather went on a drunken rampage during a card came with some relatives. He was running through the apartment, yelling, "Where's my gun? I'm going to kill the goddamn son of a bitch!" while my mother was trying to keep him from finding it. I was probably no more than eight years old, hiding under the bed, my baby sister crying in a basinet in the corner. Fortunately, the police showed up after a call from the neighbor and proceeded to calm him down, while my cousin and her husband made a quick getaway. A half-an-hour later, he was passed out on the sofa. My mother and I slept in the same bed that night. I don't know if she was able to sleep that night. I know I didn't and the memory has colored my whole attitude toward guns.

I often shared the story with my students, who were always caught off-guard by such a seedy confession from their prim and proper well-educated English teacher. I wanted them to know that I could understand where some of them were coming from, the broken family, the mom and dad who couldn't pay the bills, the one sitting there wanting to go to college but without the slightest idea of how that could ever happen.

"But what if you had to shoot somebody? What if somebody was hurting your kids or your husband? What if somebody was going to do something really bad to you? What would you do?" They wanted an honest answer.

The best I could do was say, "I don't think I could pick up a gun and point it at somebody, intending to shoot, but I don't know. I would fight for my life and the life of someone I loved, but . . . I don't want to have the option of killing another person for something that's not important, like stealing my TV set." (That was always one of the ifs they asked about. What if somebody broke into your house and was taking away your . . . whatever?")

The discussion usually ended when I said, "I don't think any person knows exactly how he or she will behave in any given set of circumstances. What I think is that whatever we know or have prepared ourselves to do in our minds with the lessons we've learned and the ideas that have influenced us, all of that together will tell us what to do and how. We just have to pray (yes, I'd say that word) that it will be the right thing, at the right time." Silence always descended upon the classroom when these little discussions took place. I tried to be honest with them, to give them the best I had to give. I hope they left with something that would see them through the hard times.

There is, however, a more terrible question for us to contemplate. What about war? Is there such a thing as "justifiable" war or "honorable" war? Didn't God allow the Israelites to use war as a means of deliverance? Isn't the Old Testament a veritable history of one war after another? What should we do when we or our sons and daughters are ordered to go to war?

Another issue closely related to the issue of war and often linked with it, is that of genocide, the systematic obliteration of a group of people, based on ethnic, racial, political or religious differences. The Pulitzer Prize winning book, *A Problem from Hell: American and the Age of Genocide* by Samantha Power, chronicles the murders of millions of people throughout the world from the Holocaust of World War II through Kosovo as examples of Power gone mad to the extent of devising unspeakable means, such as gas chambers and poison gases, as ways of eliminating those, who for one reason or another, are deemed as threats or unworthy to live. Sadly, much of the blame for these continuing atrocities lies not only with the perpetrators but also with those—such as the United States, the European Union, and the United Nations—who did not muster the moral outrage to act against murderous regimes such as Germany, Bosnia, Iraq, Rwanda, and present-day Darfur, until millions of innocents had been slaughtered. How does an individual, a nation, or the world justify its unwillingness to stop mass murder?

In a discussion concerning issues of sin and morality, a friend observed that none of the people sitting in the room had ever murdered anyone and furthermore were unlikely to do so. Without replying verbally, I asked myself this question: If we as citizens of a country pay taxes that are used as means of support in the killing of innocent people, are we guilty of murder? Conversely, if we as citizens pay taxes in support of policies that do not support the condemnation of acts of genocide or are not used in ways that take action against those who commit mass murder, are we as guilty as those who carry out the destruction of human life?

In our own country, gun-related deaths among minority young people as in gang or drug-related violence and domestic violence deaths of women and children often make headlines but provoke little outrage among the general populace. The total numbers for both types of murder must be in the thousands but because the victims are often poor, or of color, or without political power, the numbers are swept under the rug and people of good will simply look the other way, thinking "It's none of my business;" "I can't do anything about it;" or "You know how those people are." Ironically, such responses echo the responses of those, citizens and elected officials alike, who stood on the sidelines of history's darkest hours as millions met their deaths in gas chambers, in prisons of torture, in schools and churches and in villages sealed off from the outside world while the forces of evil world wreaked their havoc against God's precious children.

For all the hand-wringing and pointing of fingers as we delve into the madness of history, it seems that as human beings we just can't get enough of the killing. Since the subject is so prevalent and the means in themselves have become more obscene, gory, and beyond the imagination, let's turn the issue of murder into moneymaking ventures and call them entertainment! Whether we watch TV, go to the movies, or shop for video games, the violence depicted most often is based upon the mayhem of murder. Though the subject may be based on real-life situations that have been reported in various media outlets, most plot outlines stem from the imaginations of writers who seem obsessed with murder for the sake of pandering to our basest nature. Studies show that males, ages eighteen to twenty-four, make up the majority of "R-rated" moviegoers, with even younger males among the purchasers of video games, although those of especially graphic violence may contain an R rating as well.

For those who have known a family member, close friend or an acquaintance who has been murdered and then finds that murder fictionalized or brought to the screen as a docudrama, the revisiting of the horror and trauma of human tragedy through an entertainment marketing ploy threatens our very sense of humanity by allowing our basest instincts to rise unfettered to the surface. Those of us who have worked with young people over a long period of time can attest to the shrinking of sensibilities in the discernment of "right versus wrong."

My students were quick to defend the use of misogynistic, sadistic, or hate-filled language with this rationalization: "Just because we listen to that music or watch those actions doesn't mean that we're going to end up talking like that or doing those things."

"Yes, but," I would answer, "does the listening or the watching make you a better person in any way, or is there something you could be doing to better use your minds, such as reading your assignment or studying for the literature test?"

I would say the same thing to adults caught in the trap of "It doesn't matter if I . . . (you fill in the blank). It doesn't affect how I behave as a Christian, or Jew, or Buddhist, or whatever religion I happen to espouse." If we buy such arguments, it would seem we are walking a very broad path, rather than a straight and narrow one.

There are no easy answers to the question raised by the Sixth Commandment. Philosophers, statesmen, and writers have debated the issue of "What is murder?" since the beginning of time. Even now, there are wars, both local and international in scope, occurring in every corner of the globe. One important thing for us to consider is that all sin, defined as disobedience to God's laws, begins with the state of our hearts, travels to our minds, takes root in our thoughts, before it becomes the physical act, whether through our mouths or through the use of our bodies.

What does God think? Where does He stand? Remeber God was witness to the murder of His only Son, our Lord.

ASSESSMENT

Have you known someone who was murdered or killed accidentally through negligence, stupidity, or freakish circumstances? Does the manner or circumstance of this death affect your way of dealing with the loss? What is your definition of murder? Could you, under any circumstance, kill another human being? Have you ever been in a situation where you thought you might have to take a life in order to preserve your own? Does society in general promote the ideal of the sanctity of life? What other issues does the examination of this commandment raise for you, as an individual, as a citizen of this nation and of the world? Explain your answer. Study the Old Testament. Go to the New Testament. Find out what Jesus has to say about the subject. What does the Holy Spirit tell you?

COMMANDMENT NUMBER SEVEN:

DO NOT COMMIT ADULTERY

If the subject of murder presents us with mind-boggling dilemmas that lead us to unsatisfactory and unsustainable conclusions, the subject of adultery proves no less difficult, not to mention uncomfortable. The most public, and probably most memorable, example of an attempted discussion of adultery took place during the presidency of Jimmy Carter, when, in an interview (what was he thinking?) for *Playboy* magazine he was asked, if I recall correctly, if he had ever committed adultery.

"No," he had answered. Then he added the words that would come back to haunt him. "But I have lusted in my heart." Of course, the implication of our own imperfection follows. "Haven't we all?" we ask ourselves, as the lesson of Jesus in the New Testament evokes when a woman caught in the act of adultery is brought before him by the religious leaders for his condemnation. Jesus, drawing in the sand, turns to her accusers and asks, "Which of you without sin will cast the first stone?" We are witnesses to one of the most famous "gotcha" moments in the New Testament. As the men move away, their tails between their legs, Jesus administers a healing balm to the woman. "Go and sin no more," he tells her with loving compassion. There is no lecture, no attempt to humiliate her or destroy whatever sense of worth she may have left. He offers her simply what she needs at that moment to go on with her life, forgiveness.

Still we have to ask ourselves what God had in mind when He added Commandment Number Seven to the rules that Moses was to deliver to the Hebrews, God's chosen people. The *Oxford American Dictionary* defines adultery as "the act of voluntary sexual intercourse by a married person with someone other than his or her own spouse." The definition provides very clear, very specific language; however, the word adultery may not in itself provide the background that informs us of the intent behind the prohibition. If we back up to the verb adulterate, we find the word defined as "to make impure or poorer in quality by adding another substance, especially an inferior one."

According to the *New Bible Commentary*, previously used as a reference, this commandment "establishes a rule for a holy married life." As the family is the basis for human society and order, this commandment allows for no violation of the bond between a man and his wife. In the Judeo-Christian tradition, God instituted marriage from the beginning of man's life on this earth as a symbol of His love for His chosen people. Later, with the coming of Christ, marriage became a sacrament, attesting to the union between Christ and His church. The act of adultery, therefore, in the Old Testament becomes a symbol of the unfaithfulness of the nation of Israel to the God who created them, delivered them from bondage and led them into the land that He had promised them. With the coming of Christ, the act of adultery takes on the symbolism of the Christian's unfaithfulness in our commitment to following Jesus.

The subject makes most of us uneasy. We may or may not know someone who has been caught in the snare of adultery or who has been an unwilling partner in a relationship soiled by the act. Most of us, men and women alike, might confess to feeling drawn to someone at sometime who was not our marriage partner. Like Jimmy Carter, we may have been guilty of lusting in our hearts, although we probably stopped short of picturing ourselves in the act itself. A little flirtation is pretty harmless, after all. In fact, human beings may find themselves in flirtatious situations without realizing that it is occurring, unless someone, usually a friend, brings the behavior to our attention.

At the same time, society in general, seems to take an all-too-casual attitude towards the acting out of unfaithfulness. Recently on a movie promotion, the character of a young woman approaches a priest in his office with a problem. She is hesitant to speak, so he prods her into stating what is troubling her. She stammers out the question, "What is the current position of the Church on the issues of fornication and adultery?" Her head is turned downward; she is obviously in great discomfort.

The priest seems equally uncomfortable, but recovers quickly. "The Church's position is what is has always been," he states unequivocally. "They are sins."

She nods and stands up to leave. "Thank you, Father," she says as she extends her hand to him. "You've been a great help." Then she's out of there. How the scene fits into the plot of the movie is of no consequence, except for the fact that the scene gets our attention, as in, *Do I want to see this movie*? (The answer is, *Probably not.*) The point that comes across in the clip is that so many of us have lost or thrown away by choice the notion of sin. Still it is hopeful to note from the question posed by the young woman, that on occasion something triggers a question about our behavior that warrants an explanation or definition from someone who has the authority to deliver an answer that is honest, moral and spiritual in nature. There seems to be a great void in the ethics, what some might refer to as the discernment of right and wrong, in the various avenues of communication in our society, whether it be in the realm of entertainment, education, business, medicine, politics, religion, government, or any other entity we might consider, including the relationships inherent in marriage and the family.

Though we may not be under the strictures of the Hebrews to "protect" our bloodlines by not having physical relations with those who are deemed to be pagan or a threat to our ethnic or religious identity, we can identify with and value the concept of acting responsibly to protect the basis of our society, and all societies, the family. If a mother or father, or both, do not adhere to the traditions of faithfulness in the marriage relationship, the harms that result will extend to the children of the family, as well as to other members of the extended family.

In the United States where fifty percent of marriages fail, ministers, social workers, marriage counselors, and even talk show hosts produce a never-ending stream of books, tapes, seminars, courses, discussion groups, and retreats, all designed to underpin the sagging family structure as a way of heading off the destructive byproducts of marriages gone wrong. Many years ago in a sophomore English class, a young woman stood before the class giving a book report about a teenager whose parents had gone through divorce. Suddenly the student was overcome with emotion as she began to relate the book's plot to her own life. The other students were drawn into her misery as she began to cry while exclaiming, "Why don't they understand what they are doing to doing to their children? They put us in the middle, making us choose between them. My life has been so horrible since my parents split up, sometimes I don't even want to get up and come to school."

The class began to try to calm her with compassionate and sympathetic comments. Some even offered their own experiences with divorce as a means of letting her know that they understood her unhappiness and frustration. Being a child of divorce myself, I could identify with her anger and resentment of her parents' actions. If any good came out of such an explosive situation, it was probably in the openness and caring that was displayed for each other as we made our way from the class. The student apologized for "losing it," but also confided that reading the book and talking about it had been helpful in dealing with her long pent-up emotions.

This one true-life example provides one of the best arguments I can think of to take the seventh commandment seriously since it is evident that the root of the problem lies in the fact that society in general takes the subject of sex, and in essence the issue of marriage and fidelity, much too casually. From advertisements of performance enhancing drugs, with their explicit language relating to sexual functions, to the blatantly vulgar lyrics of popular music, and on to the constant displays of sexual activities and language on TV and in the movies (even a PG-13 rating can produce blushes), the subject of sex in all of its varieties is thrown at us from every conceivable direction twenty-four hours a day. The sexuality of young women is exploited through the merchandising of clothing, cosmetics, cigarettes, even into the area of college and professional sports with their squads of skimpily clad cheerleaders, with their gyrations and suggestive moves that would have raised the ire of their parents' and grandparents' generations.

The language used by the characters in both movies and TV series is profane, often bordering on the obscene. One example popped up recently as part of a "teaser" for CBS's *Two and a Half Men,* a show I've never watched due to the offensiveness of other "teasers" that are constantly thrown at us as the network switches from one program to another. In this one, Britney Spears, who has certainly acted out her share of unspeakable behavior, is speaking to one of the major characters, whose name I cannot remember. She coyly asks him, "Can't we have sex first and then go shopping afterward?" To which the major character answers, "I like you. You know, I really like you!" while she beams as if she has just been crowned the Queen of the Rose Bowl Parade.

That tawdry bit of what now passes as entertainment was immediately followed by a commercial for Viagra, in which a group of country and western singers tuned up and wrote right there on the spot in the recording studio a no-holds-barred romantic ditty designed to set all their back home wives, or girlfriends, into a frenzy of passion. "Viva Viagra!" sang the aging Lotharios as they strummed their trusty six-stringed guitars. Is there any wonder that TV viewing is in a sharp decline in spite of having hundreds of channels to watch? I find the commercials embarrassing to watch even with my own husband. Just when I think that the networks and their advertisers can't sink any lower, here comes another stupid, irresponsible, blatantly offensive advertisement and it's all I can do not to heave the nearest weighty object straight at the TV screen. As a result, our TV screen is turned off probably seventy-five to ninety percent of the time.

There seem to be no restrictions placed on behaviors, sexual innuendo, references to bodily functions, or even irreverent references to God or Jesus. In other words, the bulldozers of amorality and the belief that "anything goes" have flattened the barriers of decency, morality, respect, and even reverence. Where are the voices calling us to examine this lackadaisical attitude toward the profane that threatens to take us down the road of complacency and self-destruction? M. Scott Peck chides us for the sins of laziness, pride and fear. Along with that, he derides our tendency towards "simplistic thinking" which is basically not thinking at all because it's too much work.

There are many who would say that adultery occurs because marriage is too much work, because people fall out of love or that they weren't right for each other to begin with, or because monogamy isn't realistic anyway. The list goes on and on, but these are simply stated rationalizations and, as I learned many years ago in a college sociology class, people can rationalize about anything they choose, and they do.

No matter how we try, the commandments will not go away. They are still there, in the second book of the Hebrew Bible, and on display in many churches and synagogues around the world. No one is more or less absolute than the other nine. We can't pick and choose which ones we will obey or not obey, although we do so every day of our lives. One may make us more uncomfortable that the others. There may be one or more than we are sure we have never disobeyed and will never disobey.

The seventh commandment opens the door to so many related questions. What about people who have been divorced? Should the church sanction marriages between divorced persons, whether one or both are divorced? How do we fix what's wrong with marriage so our families and society are not threatened by the fallout of the after effects of all these toxic relationships? The only thing that seems certain is that there are no easy answers and that we have plenty of work, considering the temptations that bombard us daily, to keep our minds clear and attuned to God's will for the sake of our families and for our civilization as well.

ASSESSMENT

What is your definition of adultery? Do you know of families that have been damaged or broken apart by this behavior? Can you identify with President Carter's "confession" in any way? How do you view our society's attitudes toward issues related to sexual behaviors? Are there specific examples that bother you or make you uncomfortable? Do you believe that religious institutions are effective in educating their congregations about the issues that relate to this commandment?

COMMANDMENT NUMBER EIGHT:

DO NOT TAKE WHAT DOES NOT BELONG TO YOU

THERE IS PROBABLY NO PERSON alive who could honestly say, "I've never taken anything that didn't belong to me." After all, most of us as children (I'm speaking here as someone who was once a child, someone who has children of her own, and also as someone who was a high school teacher with rooms filled with other people's children) had no trouble whatsoever getting into trouble by taking things that belonged to their classmates.

In fact, a memory of one of my first days as a substitute teacher surfaced as I finished the previous sentence. I was in a class of twenty or more second grade children when one of the students informed me that "Charles was picking on Bobby" and, on top of that, had taken all of Bobby's crayons. The other students quickly turned to look at the two boys who sat next to each other in the very back of the room. Charles was shaking his head at me as if to say, "There's no way she could be talking about me," while Bobby, who looked for all the world like a tiny, shriveled up prune, sat with his head hanging low, sniffling loud enough for the whole world to hear. The children, held in the throes of a still segregated education system, turned and fixed their gazes on me, clearly wondering, "How is this pathetic little white woman going to fix this mess?"

As I stood to ask Bobby what had happened, "Charles" stood up and began moving to the back corner of the room. "Please don't hit me, Miss Stump," he begged, and with good reason, because for the past two days, he had done all he could to aggravate every child in the class, not to mention his totally overwhelmed substitute teacher.

"I'm not going to hit you, Charles," I assured him calmly, even as I conjured up the image of a black belt that lay inside the top desk drawer. I could never spank my own children; it was unbelievable to me, although the teacher next door had given me permission to "show them who's boss if necessary," that I would administer corporal punishment to someone else's child. In the meantime, Bobby was blubbering away, while the rest of the children whispered and wiggled in anticipation of a highly entertaining showdown between the white lady and her nemesis of the past two days.

"Bobby, did Charles take your crayons?" I asked. He nodded as the rest of the class shook their heads in agreement.

"Charles, I'm going to give you one last chance to tell the truth. If you return Bobby's crayons and apologize to him and to the class for disrupting their lessons, that will be the end of this. If you don't, I suppose I'll have to use Ms. Reading's belt." I began to open the top drawer.

Charles started wailing and moving about the room, begging me not to whip him, all the while proclaiming, "I didn't do nuttin' to Bobby. I didn't take his crayons," as the children confronted him with cries of "You did, too. We saw you. You're one big liar." I was beginning to get a headache as I headed back to Charles, the belt in my hand. Now, when did I pick that up? I wondered to myself.

I reached out to grab Charles's arm, but he was so big I

couldn't catch hold of him. My hand flashed the belt toward him, but he was turning from me, pulling me with him. The room became deadly silent. I was on the verge of humiliation, a grown woman being bested by a second grader, albeit one of gargantuan size! I managed one feeble slap at Charles's rear which caused him to bellow like a wounded bull. The children cheered, Bobby reached into Charles's desk and grabbed his crayons, just as the bell rang for school to be dismissed. Charles literally ran for the door while the "little Miss Perfects" gathered around me to tell me that Charles had it coming, and they were glad I had been their teacher for three days. When everyone had left, I sat down exhausted, almost in tears. Three days hard work down the drain, I thought, all because an oversized second grader decided to steal the crayons of a classmate who would never have the guts to put up a fight. Such is the way of the world, I thought. No wonder God decided to put it in His top ten commandments for getting along with Him and each other.

We're all guilty. As children, we took the cookies from the cookie jar, borrowed Mama's best sweater or Dad's favorite tie, sneaked our big sister's skates or our brother's bike, just for a little while. They weren't around; they wouldn't miss the record, the ball, or the new bracelet. After all, we're family, right? That's what families are for, to share each other's treasures. We don't ask because they'll probably say, "No," not because it really matters so much, as it is for the perversity of having the power to withhold something they know we really want.

So on it goes. As teenagers we "borrow" a friend's car. That happened to me and one of my college roommates, when two fellows invited us to go to a neighboring town to get pizza, a real novelty in the '50s. What we didn't know was that our friends had taken their roommate's car without his permission, a fact that did not surface until two hours later, when the car, which was being driven way too fast, headed off the road on a curve into a tree because we were trying to beat the deadline for getting back to the dorm. Only then did the boys tell us that they had, you know, "borrowed" the car. Well, it was their problem! One of the fraternity boys and his date stopped and offered us a lift to the dorm, so we left the fellows to work it out the best that they could. After all, it wasn't our idea to head over the county line for pizza in a stolen car. We just went along for the ride.

Misbehavior has a way of starting with small things. At work, maybe we grab a handful of paper clips or rubber bands; next thing we know we're taking the ball point pens and staplers.

I'm sure many teenagers started their shoplifting careers by taking a dare from a friend for something that was thought to be insignificant, such as a candy bar or a pack of gum. One of my students stated in class that almost everyone he knew had shoplifted something at some time, and the rest of the class nodded in agreement, some of them smiling sheepishly while proclaiming themselves guilty. I immediately informed them that shoplifting costs companies billions of dollars each year and that we as consumers had to recoup the losses by paying higher prices for the products that we buy.

One girl told the class that she had tried to steal a tee shirt at the beach while she was shopping with her dad and that he had caught her. "I was so embarrassed, but my dad didn't yell or scream at me. He apologized to the owner and gave me a good lecture when we left, telling me how I had disappointed him. It made me realize how important it was to live up to my parents' expectations because they had done so much for me. I've never stolen another thing because I know it's not worth the hurt it would cost my parents."

The analogy is clear. God is our father and we are His children. He isn't going to yell and scream when we disobey His commandments, but He certainly takes us aside and gives us a good talking-to. He has higher expectations for us and has spelled them out for us in the Ten Commandments, which are not a bunch of irrational old fuddy-duddy rules. There is a sound foundation of logical reasoning behind each one. Just as God seeks to establish a relationship with each one of us on a very personal basis, we should wish to establish a relationship with each of our fellow human beings.

If we act in ways, however, that cause distrust and even possible harm, we will be guilty of destroying these relationships and with them, our relationship to the God who has called us to a higher level of commitment, not only to Him, but to our brothers and sisters who share this planet with us. Sin disrupts the relationship and causes us to be isolated from one another. The isolation leads to further sin and thus we find ourselves in an endless cycle of broken relationships. This is the lesson of Nathaniel Hawthorne's masterpiece, *The Scarlet Letter*. The hidden sins of the three major characters bring not only pain and isolation to their individual lives but also great harm to each other and to the innocent child who connects them. Hawthorne shows us that stealing may extend beyond mere possessions into the realm of the intangible, such as "stealing" a person's good name or livelihood, even a person's innocence or virtue, all to satisfy the desire for vengeance.

In everyday life, "minor" examples of thievery run rampant: the "theft" of a person's good name through injurious gossip; the "theft" of uncollected taxes by those who underpay workers, or by the workers themselves who accept wages "under the table." Most of us who scrutinize our actions carefully will find that we have at one time or another taken what did not belong to us with the rationalization that the item did not appear to have an owner. I have collected bags of gourds from an unplanted field where the seeds of last year's crop produced hundreds of "volunteers" that appeared but with no obvious attempt at harvest as the field was left unplowed and unplanted for the new season. I have also picked up cabbages and pumpkins, usually the lower grade ones, that were left behind after their finer brothers and sisters had been collected to send off to market. After all, the dregs of the gourd and pumpkin society were just lying there, rotting away. Why not take these poor misshapen, underdeveloped castaways home to brighten the doorway and entrance to our mountain home during the Thanksgiving season? There were no signs that proclaimed "No Trespassing" or "Pay at the red house down the road." If so, I would have counted out my money and paid with a grateful heart and a smile. But the trucks are gone and the fields are bare, except for the imperfects, left waiting for the deer or the frost, whichever comes first to perform its part in recycling the remnants left behind. I am a gleaner, I tell myself; where is the harm?

Just as "a slip of a lip may sink a ship," the taking of one insignificant item may well be a factor in the ultimate destruction of one's own character. "So way leads on to way," Robert Frost reminds us; or, in the words of young people discussing the lessons of literature, "What goes around comes around."

In our society, thievery has almost been elevated to an art form. The news is filled with stories of the theft of valuable masterpieces from famous museums. There are the reports of the theft of billions of dollars from taxpayers by defense contractors, the stealing from the federal government in the form of underreported earnings by both individuals and companies that hide their profits in off shore accounts. Most of us know at least one person who has been victimized by identify theft, not to mention the potential threat of the same tactics used by terrorists and political assassins.

Politicians "steal" money from public coffers to pay for prostitutes, not to mention such items as luxury automobiles, jewelry, foreign travel, and the list goes on. John Grisham's latest book is based on the premise that special interests, in the form of big businesses, insurance companies, with a little help from their elected representatives, can "steal" an election from an honest, hard working public servant. Though Grisham is careful to emphasize that the novel is fiction, he also lets us know in his afterword that the elements that produce the "right" candidate for the job are out there waiting to be bought in various and sundry under the radar deals, so the basic aspects of the plot should not be tossed aside as the overactive imagination of a writer.

When we see how far the breaking of one commandment can take us, in terms of destruction to individuals and to society as a whole, we gain insight into the rationale behind the rules that God has placed in our classroom of life. Our sins have a way of snowballing themselves into avalanches of destruction. To paraphrase the title of one of our favorite old sitcoms, *Father Knows Best*, our Father does know best and we ought to spend a lot more time listening to what He has to say.

ASSESSMENT

Have you ever found yourself contemplating taking something that did not belong to you? Do you think it is easy to dismiss some of our actions that are in essence theft as of no particular consequence? Do you know someone whose life has been changed dramatically by stealing, either as the victim or the perpetrator? How do you see our society as perhaps as enabler in the problem of taking that which belongs to someone else? Have you established "rules" for yourself and your family as to your attitudes and behaviors concerning taking what does not belong to you?

COMMANDMENT NUMBER NINE:

DON'T GIVE FALSE TESTIMONY AGAINST YOUR NEIGHBOR

SOMETIMES IT IS EASY FOR us to remember that the term neighbor as used in both the Old Testament and later by Jesus in his story regarding the good Samaritan applies to every man, woman and child who inhabits this planet along side each of us. It is, therefore, incumbent upon us as citizens of God's kingdom to avoid any defamation of any person's character, not only in a court of law but also in other legal proceedings, such as in the taking of a deposition. Furthermore, the prohibition of false testimony extends into the realm of the everyday, outside the boundaries of legal ramifications.

Deuteronomy 5–20 reinforces the prohibition. Although commandments, each one presents the positive action by contrasting the false testimony against testimony that is honest and truthful. In other words, we are to act in contrast to the commandment's telling us what *not* to do.

If we are followers of Jesus who is the Way, the Truth, and the Light, we must always bear witness to the truth, whether in the courtroom, in our Sunday school class, or at a meeting of the bridge club. How simple the application seems! The dilemma comes when one person's perception conflicts with another's. An example comes from the students who passed through my classroom over the course of more than thirty years. Most of them, I can truthfully state, respected me and held me in high regard, even to the point of reciting en masse on occasion, "We love you, Mrs. Stump." (Music to any teacher's ears.) There were individuals, however, who openly detested me and sought to do anything or everything to make my life miserable. Under his breath, he thought, I heard one young man refer to me as "the witch." Of course, the epithet could have been worse. Others went out of their way to poison the minds of those who followed on their paths the next semester. One day, when I was energetically trying to draw a humorous response as a means of underscoring a point in a discussion on a piece of literature, one student raised her hand and proclaimed, "They (whoever that might have been) told us you were so hard and difficult to get along with. You're not like that at all." In other words, someone along the way has given a "false" testimony in terms of who I am and how I behave.

"Well," I explained, "if you follow the rules and do your work, there will never be a problem between us, but for those who can't or won't behave responsibly, I guess I can come down pretty hard." It isn't hard to discern the analogy of a teacher and the rules she lays out for her students as applying to God and the commandments He has given to His chosen people, including that of not defaming another person's character or name.

In our society, it's evident that there are individuals who don't want to know the rules. Even if they are aware of the rules that are supposed to govern the game of life, whether in the moral or legal realm, they refuse to abide by them, making the choice of going their own way until circumstances or authorities must intervene to stop them from doing damage not only to themselves but to society in general. Name calling, using derogatory terminology, misrepresentation of the facts, and other facets of dealing with others using dishonest and misleading tactics have become too commonplace throughout major institutions of our society. One has only to recall recent scandals on the national level, such as in the world of business, politics, government, and even religion, to realize that Truth is not only enigmatic but easily discarded by those whose self-interests take priority.

Think of the trials we've watched, either from real life or in the realm of fictional movies or TV series. As the trial moves forward, testimony is elicited from both the plaintiff and the defendant. There is one event or set of events that has brought this case to trial, yet we hear two conflicting sets of testimony, often so diverse, so broad in discrepancies, we wonder if we are not witnessing two separate trials that are taking place simultaneously. We make judgments about who is telling the truth and who is lying. We listen to the evidence and are sure that this is an open and shut case. We listen to lawyers who often ridicule or disparage with great disrespect the testimony offered up on the opposing side. What is the truth, we wonder, and how will it ever come to light of day?

Perhaps the greatest dilemma we face as Christians is discerning the truth of God's message to His world, considering the endless pronouncements concerning theology, faith and witness that are hurled at us by those who proclaim to be His messengers and followers of Jesus Christ. The only truth that can be derived from the content and delivery of those who represent denominational interests as well as independently operated institutions of worship and outreach is that no one individual or church, whether local or tied to a national or international "body of Christ" has determined to focus on the One Truth that has the power to bring us together with a common purpose, the truth that Jesus is Lord. Once Christians make that commitment their Universal Mission Statement and let all the other theological debates fall by the wayside, we may be on our way to winning the world for Christ.

ASSESSMENT

How easy, or difficult, is it to tell the truth? What factors make "knowing or learning the truth" such hard work? Have you ever been guilty of "bearing false witness" against another person? Were there repercussions? Do others recognize you as an honest person, a truth teller? What aspects of society do you think are representative of "shading" or misrepresenting the truth? What role does integrity play in obedience to the ninth commandment?

COMMANDMENT NUMBER TEN:

DO NOT DESIRE THOSE THINGS THAT BELONG TO OTHERS

RECENTLY IN THE LITTLE CHURCH that we attend when we are in residence at our mountain home, the pastor took time to greet visitors before the service began. As he addressed one couple that attends the second church that he pastors, he noted that they had arrived in a bright, shiny red sports car that he very much admired. "Of course, I'm not supposed to covet your car," he joked as he laughed along with his audience, "but I can honestly say that I wouldn't mind having one exactly like it!" His observation reminds us that this is the distinction we have been taught to make in our yearnings for those things others have that, in all probability, we can't or won't obtain because of obstacles or circumstances beyond our control.

If we are honest, we will admit that we have been guilty far too often of coveting what belongs to someone else. In all likelihood, however, as adults we have never gone so far as to steal another person's jewelry, car or money; although we have become green with envy when we have been on the sidelines, privy to the exchange of extravagant gifts or watching friends shop with seemingly no limit on what can be purchased, whether by cash or credit card. If we are honest, we will admit that we have envied others not only for their material possessions, but for the intangibles as well, such as professional success or an award or citation of recognition by the community. Coveting something that belongs to someone else may not result in outright thievery, but the "thought" could very well take us down a road of certain behaviors that leads to other unethical or immoral behaviors, such as manipulation, fraud, deceit, and other kinds of dishonesty that indirectly imply the theft of other intangibles, including dishonoring another's name or good standing, stealing a person's identity (all too common these days), even to the point of taking someone's livelihood through gossip and innuendo.

It is intriguing to note how closely the idea of envy and wanting what another has is tied to the grand old American game of advertising. Spend some time analyzing the messages sent across the airways by everything from soup to soap and beyond. The bottom line is that "everyone" has this, does that, drives so and so, watches such and such and the beat goes on. Advertisers are in the business of making us to want what our neighbors have, even if those neighbors are way out of our socioeconomic circles. We go so far as to listen to the advice of celebrities in the realms of sports and entertainment, as if we actually believe their life choices regarding the cars they drive, the medicines they take, or the cosmetics they use would have any impact whatsoever on the course of our very ordinary lives. We are left to wonder how many young people have been led astray to a path of addiction or crime by one simple temptation, the desire to be like ________, complete with clothing, house, car, jewelry, etc. Over the many years that I was a high school teacher, I heard many students express the idea of following in the footsteps of some athlete or rock star, so that "I can have lots of money and do whatever I want."

As children it is probable that at one time or another we

took something that belonged to a playmate or a school friend without thinking of the action as something very bad or forbidden. The same is equally true for the other nine commandments. A large part of our reaction to life's rules obviously lies in whether or not we know what they are, how significant or effective the consequences that have occurred when the rules have been violated, and the extent to which the individual can let his or her conscience be a twenty-four hour on-call guide. The last provision takes on even more importance when we recognize the truth that some consciences seem to be more highly developed than others. For some children, taking a dollar or two out of Dad's wallet will be seen as "no big deal." For others, the slightest step out of the path of obedience to right over wrong may result in a confession before the transgression is even discovered!

The patterns involving the discernment of right over wrong usually continue throughout a person's lifetime and have great impact on the relationships that are part and parcel of who we are and what we do with our lives, whether they involve our family, our friends, our education, our vocation, our recreation or our spiritual life as played out in a religious contest. Those who have a lackadaisical attitude toward playing by the rules often run into trouble with moral and legal ramifications, taking innocent bystanders along with them as they spiral out of control.

A recent get together with several couples with whom we had a working and living relationship on a child care facility many years ago reminded me of an incident with the youngest son of one of our friends. There was a day care center on the campus and, during the course of their youth, most of the children attended the kindergarten. One day, the father walked outside during his lunch hour at his home and found his five-year-old son sitting on the porch steps. Calling the child by name, he asked, "Billy (not his real name), what are you doing home from kindergarten? It's only twelve o'clock. School is out at 2:30."

Billy looked straight at his father and proclaimed, "Rules, rules, rules. That's all I hear. I just couldn't take it any longer so when recess came, I decided to come home!" Billy, however, had a lesson coming. His father took him by the hand and led him back to his classroom; in addition Billy was prodded into an apology to his teacher who had become frantic when she discovered one of her students had gone AWOL. As his father was leaving, Billy couldn't resist having the last word. "You can make me come back, but I still won't like being here one bit."

Unfortunately, I've witnessed the same behaviors in my own classroom. There are some students for whom rules simply don't apply, and they have no hesitancy in telling you so, not to mention the fact that their obstinacy is based on parental teachings. More than once I've had students stand up and tell me, "My mama said that nobody can tell me that I have to do something that I don't want to." Oh, dear. Is that what Mama said, or what you thought Mama said, or what you just made up along the way? Whatever. The bottom line is that one day this blatant disregard for authority will cost her in an unimaginable way; the failure to be admitted to her chosen school, the loss of a job, and failure of a marriage, even her ability to make it in a world controlled by rules, whether they are deemed fair or not.

So what does this have to do with the subject of the tenth commandment? One commentary points out the last commandment as the foundation of the previous four commandments. By revisiting them, we note that what they have in common concerns our actions toward our fellow human beings. We *shall not* take another's life; we *shall not* violate our marriage vows, thus bringing harm to the family and society; we *shall not* steal another person's property; we *shall not* bring dishonor to the name or character of our neighbor. The "shall nots" are imperatives pronounced by God. We do not make our own rules for behavior on this earth; He has provided them for us to revere and obey. While these prohibitions involve our actions, the acting in opposition of what we are told not to do, the tenth commandment focuses on our thoughts, from which all our actions flow. It is the lack of control in our thought processes that takes us away from God and down our own path to the actions that are sinful and cause so much harm to the world. One small step off the path can have disastrous consequences, which is why it is so important to constantly revisit God's Ten Commandments and reevaluate our actions on a regular basis.

ASSESSMENT

Do you have a clear definition of covetousness that you adhere to? Where and how do you think this "sin" originates? Have you ever or do you now envy another person in any way insofar as possessions or personal attributes are concerned? What steps are you taking to rid yourself of thoughts that involve the issue of wanting something that someone else has? Have you ever experienced distasteful consequences as a result of envy? What actions or plan can you take to alleviate the envies that exist in your life?

EPILOGUE

AS WE DROVE UP THE mountain yesterday, I spotted high on the ridge above me a glimpse of this year's first trilliums. How time flies. The old adage floated past my brain and I was suddenly reminded of last spring's strange encounter with the God of the Flame Azalea and the commission He had given to me, which I have somewhat dutifully attended to between all the comings and goings of my life. Probably not what He had in mind, but I have stuck with the task and tried to do my best, although I am not convinced that we humans ever come close to the being and the doing of such.

Today I am headed out for what I hope will be a reunion with my favorite flame azalea, if I can find it, and another earthly encounter with God, which actually happens every day, but I, like most of us, just go on my own way not paying much attention to the heavenly mysteries that surround us. (I know that flame azaleas don't bloom when dogwoods and trilliums do, but as my grandson at age five once reminded me, "Oh, yeah, God, well He's magic!")

As I gather the gear for my adventure, which includes dog biscuits, carrots for horses, my iPod and walking stick, my husband follows me out into the yard as I search for Princess, my faithful adopted dog. "Where are you headed this time?" I always let him know the direction I am taking, although I will confess that I have on occasion changed my mind, leaving myself vulnerable to the unexpected with no hope of rescue. (Sound familiar?)

"Up Doe Run to Groundhog, maybe across the Parkway to the old logging road. I won't be gone over an hour."

"Uh huh," he answers, "Your hours have a way of turning into two or three, especially if you stop to talk with one of the neighbors along the way."

I hope so, I am thinking, but I don't give myself away. "Of course, I'll probably stop and give Ginger and Blackie a treat or try to get Ledford's horses to come to the fence, but you'll know where I'm headed if the weather changes. I should be back no later than four. (I give myself an extra forty-five minutes just in case.) I turn back and wave as Princess runs up alongside of me and moves ahead as she watches me turn toward the Parkway.

The day is sunny and warm, with dogwoods and redbuds treating us to splotches of pastels peeking through the gold tinged new leaves of spring. The winding road runs free of cars, bikes and motorcycles. Princess and I are alone, but not lonely, amidst the splendor of mountain magnolias and hidden treasures of bloodroot and white trilliums, some already turning the pink with age that signals old age. I hum along with James Taylor as he sings, "Shower the people you love with love," thinking of a recent funeral for one of our son's high school buddies where the song was played at the close of the service. Life is short and very uncertain, I think to myself as I focus on the beauty that envelops me in its soft cocoon, trying to ignore the aches and pains of my own aging limbs. Even so, I keep on walking, walking, walking to the beat of James Taylor's drummer, as I remind myself that I need the exercise not only for my body but for my mind and soul as well.

In no time at all, I have reached the Parkway and am ready to begin the search for the Sacred Flaming Azalea, believing I am headed in the right direction but perhaps not so sure after all. Billions and billions of worn, soggy leaves have covered the tracks of the old logging road and I am soon almost up to my shins in their remains, all the while telling myself that it is too early for snakes to be out, but what if they could not resist the first heady whiffs of spring air and have abandoned all of nature's laws in favor of their own independence? I rake my walking stick into the hidden ruts, knocking against the ground as I go, willing the vibrations to send them not only from my sight but from my mind as well.

I find it difficult to keep on a straight course because I am overcome with the drunkenness of one who has imbibed too much of nature's liquor; the breathtaking colors of birds in flights, the heartbreaking music of their courtships, the sneak peeks of multi-hued violets and trailing arbutus. I consult my watch. I have already frittered away forty minutes of my promised-to-return-within-time with no flame azalea in sight. I look around and realize I am in unfamiliar territory. I cannot hear the sounds of cars traveling the parkway or see through the thickets of rhododendron that surround me to anything that resembles a house or barn or even a fence. Blackberry and wild rose brambles pull and tug at my sweatshirt and jeans. Princess has disappeared from sight and the woods closing in on me are suddenly overshadowed with dark clouds. Oh, dear. I didn't think to bring the cell phone. Again. One of these days I will learn, I tell myself as I begin to turn in a circle, trying to get my bearings. Do I turn back and try to retrace my steps in the leaves or press on hoping to come upon a familiar path or landmark?

I'm too old to be so stupid, I scold myself.

"You certainly are," a voice answers. "And to think I gave you the job of updating my Commandments. Oh, well. It's only the second time I've made a mistake. Of course, if you count both Adam and Eve, it would be the third."

I turn in the direction of The Voice, while trying to decide which actor has an almost identical voice, same delivery, intonation . . .

"You're probably thinking of Charlton Heston," He offers.

"No, I don't think so. He played Moses, remember? Well, of course, You remember because You don't forget anything, do you?"

"Actually, I do. I forget your sins if you ask. You remember that about me, don't you?"

"Of course, I remember. It's just that . . . we sometimes have a hard time forgiving ourselves, so we forget that you forgave us first. That is, if we asked. Do people always ask for your forgiveness?"

"No, they don't, which makes for a lot of problems for the human race. I'm waiting around, throwing hints right down in front of people. Just say you're sorry, I keep telling them. I'll forgive you. It's very simple. Two little words—three, if you don't use the contraction—but too many of you haven't grown up yet. You act like children. You have to be begged or threatened or coerced, but you see, I don't do those things. I put it right out there; no strings, no false advertising. You do or you don't. It's up to you. Maybe that was mistake number three, or four, but who's counting?"

"The azalea is even more beautiful than last year," I offer, hoping to change the subject.

"I don't think it's possible to truly compare one beauty to another. That's why there are so many varieties of living things in the world. People shouldn't spend their time comparing deer to turkeys or robins to grosbeaks. The uniqueness of each organism, whether it is a snowflake or diamond, contains the building blocks of creation. The same is true of each human being."

"It makes me sad that so many people ignore nature and take it for granted. They never seem to pay attention. I could watch goldfinches fly from sunrise to sunset and never become bored with their brilliant colors or the marvelous way they fly, almost like grasshoppers who have taken to the sky."

"You're rhyming again. You did that a lot when you were teaching and even once in a while when you're just carrying on an ordinary conversation."

"You don't know how hard it was for me not to lapse into poetry when I was revisiting your Commandments!?"

"I'm certainly aware of your efforts and I hope you have been aware of my presence along the way, but I'm no critic. There are all kinds of inspirations in this world. I've been with you, helping you sort out and select from what you know intellectually and feel spiritually, but I'm not a puppet maker or ventriloquist. Your choices are your own. Once you are satisfied that you have done your best at what I've asked you to do, you're free to take the next step. It's up to you; make your revisions, ask a friend or friends to offer comments or suggestions. Every task must come to an end. When you are ready, the world will be ready for you.

"It sounds easy, but on the other hand, more difficult than I imagined."

"The important thing is that I asked you to do something and you've taken me seriously. Few people do. In the meantime, I think you should head back to the house. You're over your time limit and Bob is getting ready to come looking for you. Princess is just over the rise to the left. The Parkway is beyond and you'll be near the Gunnysack crossing. If you start now, you'll meet him just as he starts up Groundhog Mountain."

"Thank for the directions. I mean in more ways than one."

"I know you do."

"And I know that You know." I laugh at my foolish attempt to make sense of the events of the past hour. As I get my bearings, I turn one last time to look at the sun's bright beams turning the azaleas into flames of red and gold.

"Not to contradict You," I call out, "but in the immortal words of my granddaughter, "isn't that about the most beautifulest thing you ever did see?"

At the bottom of the hill, a car is waiting for me. Rolling down the window, my husband asks, "Do you know how long you've been gone? Where have you been?"

"Off in the woods," I tease, "talking to a big old flame azalea. I found it last year and wanted to see if I could find it again and if it was in bloom. It's so huge it must have been here a long, long time. If it could talk, I'm sure it would have a lot to say."

"I imagine so," he answers tersely. "Do you want to ride back or walk? It's almost five o'clock." He is an avid teller of time.

"I'll walk," I answer as Princess runs up along side of me. "You never know. There just might be another flame azalea hiding in these woods and I wouldn't want to miss whatever it has to show me."

He turns the car around and heads home. I stand under the shade of the trees, looking slowly about me, trying to take in the lessons nature has written on her lovely pages. I won't ever learn it all, I think, but the least I can do is to keep watching and listening. I move on down Doe Run, taking in the vision of green fields in habited by black cows and calves and in the distance, the great purple outline of Buffalo Mountain.

What will I do with the manuscript that is stored on my

trusty flash drive? I think of the words of wisdom pronounced by the good professor who guided me through my master's thesis and encouraged me to keep on writing. "Have you ever thought, Phyllis, that what you most fear is not failure, but success?" The world's definition of success matters little to me, which is why I seem lacking in ambition, but measuring up to God's expectations for me keeps me on the edge of where do I go from here and is this a part of God's will for my life?

Why did He speak to me and place this idea of revisiting His Commandments through the context of the society and the times in which we live? For me, there is only one answer: to share with others what He has placed in my heart and given me the gift to communicate. As the psalmist has written, "Great peace have those who love Your law." Grant us the grace to love your Law, dear Lord, that your peace may abide with us forever.

Amen.

ABOUT THE AUTHOR

After teaching English in several North Carolina high schools for over thirty years, then serving in a part time administrative position for the following six tears, Phyllis Stump found a new career portraying Orlen(a) Puckett, a legendary midwife in the area around Patrick and Carroll County, Virginia. Puckett's cabin is located near milepost 189.5 on the Blue Ridge Parkway. Several times each summer Phyllis transforms herself into the nearly 100 year old midwife who carried twenty-four babies and helped deliver over 1000 babies in this area without losing a mother or baby. She has also performed in theatres, retirement homes, churches and given fund raisers in five states. She can be reached by email at bpstump@lexcominc.net.

She resides in Lexington, North Carolina, with her husband Bob and maintains an "off the Blue Ridge Parkway home" in Carroll County, Virginia. In August, 2009, she suffered a massive bleed on the left side of her brain but since has made a miraculous comeback. She has published two books of poetry, *The Heart Knows* and *Walking the Gunnysack Trail,* along with two novels, *Called: The Story of a Mountain Midwife* and *Millennium,* and a work of nonfiction, *Catch a Falling Star: The Stories that Test Scores Don't Tell.*

Phyllis and her husband have three children and six grandchildren, plus a multitude of hobbies including reading, painting, gardening and crafts. They have also been involved in mission work in China, Brazil, and Belize with an emphasis on working with children.

She has a BA from UNC–Greensboro and a Master of Arts in Liberal Studies from Wake Forest University where she completed the novel *Pictures from the Past Imperfect* as part of her master's thesis.

www.ingramcontent.com/pod-product-compliance
Lightning Source LLC
Chambersburg PA
CBHW030944090426
42737CB00007B/529
* 9 7 8 1 9 3 6 9 1 2 0 4 9 *